Praise F

Chasing Jesus

"Cassie Downs takes her readers on a 60-day adventure that is sure to leave you laughing out loud, crying, and hungry for more of God. Each devotional is practical, thought-provoking, and will, without a doubt, make you want to chase after Jesus."

— BEAU NORMAN, PASTOR, *THE HILL CHURCH.*

"Cassie has a way with words that meet the every-day woman right where she is. From typical day jobs to baking brownies, her devotions go straight to the heart. I could definitely relate to the devotions about comparison. It's just what my soul needed to be refreshed and reminded that I am not alone in this struggle. It's so comforting that Cassie writes so openly about her struggles so we can relate to them. You'll find yourself wrapped up in the words that offer daily praise and prayer. The prayers go from a burdened woman into the ears of an all-knowing God whom the writer finds complete solace and comfort in. These are words and prayers that we need to live by."

— SAMANTHA CABRERA, AUTHOR OF *ALL IS GRACE.*

"*Chasing Jesus* is packed with both practical and power-filled ways to live out your God-given purpose! Prepare to be encouraged and loved as Cassie points you to Jesus day after day."

— JENNY RANDLE, SPEAKER, AUTHOR OF *COURAGEOUS CREATIVE*,
PODCAST CO-HOST OF *SHUT THE SHOULD UP.*

"Cassie Downs has an incredible way of encouraging you in your daily walk with the LORD. She uses every day, every situation, applications to urge you to WALK BOLDLY with JESUS. I cannot wait to get Chasing Jesus into the hands of the women in our ministry! Chasing Jesus is an AMAZING book to train up women to LIVE authentically for CHRIST!"

— MIS KEITH, FOUNDER OF *SOULFIRE MINISTRIES.*

"Chasing Jesus will open your heart and encourage you to continue your personal journey toward peace in your life. Cassie Downs will help you discover your own path to faith with her honest and homespun style of writing."

— *AMBER HORNBECK, STAFF WRITER AT*
THE DAILY AMERICAN REPUBLIC

CHASING JESUS

CHASING JESUS

A 60 day devotional

Cassie Downs

ELM HILL

A Division of
HarperCollins Christian Publishing

www.elmhillbooks.com

Chasing Jesus

Published in Nashville, Tennessee, by Elm Hill, an imprint of Thomas Nelson. Elm Hill and Thomas Nelson are registered trademarks of HarperCollins Christian Publishing, Inc.

www.cassiedowns.com

Elm Hill titles may be purchased in bulk for educational, business, fund-raising, or sales promotional use. For information, please e-mail SpecialMarkets@ ThomasNelson.com.

Library of Congress Cataloging-in-Publication Data

Library of Congress Control Number: 2020904791

ISBN 978-0-310116271 (Paperback)
ISBN 978-0-310116295 (eBook)

To Annah,
Be a woman unafraid to live every moment,
chasing Jesus and spreading His love everywhere you go.

In loving memory of my grandparents
who have chased Jesus into eternity.
May I leave a legacy as great as yours.

Jerry Reynolds
Jim and Dianne Bowman
Luther and Lousie Bowman
Rose Brown

CONTENTS

INTRODUCTION

Hey, friend! My name is Cassie, and I wanted to share a little about me before you dive into Chasing Jesus. I'm 16 years blissfully married to my hottie of a hubs, Dustin. Together we have the honor of serving as operations pastors at our home church. Along with the ministry at The Hill Church, I am the founder and president of Everyday Jesus Ministry. This girl loves to communicate at churches and events. Anytime I write or speak about Jesus, it's a good day! If that isn't a full plate, together Dustin and I have three kiddos who I homeschool: Wyatt age 15 (my rebel public schooler), Annah 13, and Tyler 11.

Enough with the serious stuff, here are a few fun facts about ya girl. I LOVE tacos and pepperoni pizza. Current River runs through my veins, and I am Hawaiian at heart. My hometown of Ellsinore, Missouri is forever a part of me and when I get away, it's the first place I run. While in Ellsinore or anywhere near water, I enjoy camping and kayaking. Oh, and did I mention my slight obsession with flowers? Well, there's that too.

****

Why Chasing Jesus? I wrote this book for one reason. YOU. You, my friend, are the reason this book is in print. Life is hard, and a life without surrender to Jesus is even harder. So, I wrote this book to encourage you.

I believe that throughout the pages ahead, you will find a desire for

Jesus unlike anything you've ever encountered. I wish so much that we could grab a glass of sweet tea or maybe a lemonade (I don't do coffee) and chat about the pages to follow. Since I can't be with you in the flesh, I vow to be with you in spirit, praying and believing incredible things for you.

God has given you so much purpose sweet friend, but with so *great* a purpose first comes a *great* relationship with Him. And that's what each of these stories will encourage. An everyday, ever-present relationship with the Lord. A life spent chasing Jesus in all that you do.

Luke 9:23 says, "*Then he said to them all, If anyone wants to follow after me, let him deny himself, take up his cross daily, and follow me,*" (CSB).

Our world offers so many things for us to chase; fame, fortune, love, power, and approval to name a few. But God has called us to deny our desires and to spend each day chasing Him and His heart for us. Each day, in every decision, in the way we walk and talk, in the way we work, in our relationships, in EVERYTHING. *Chase Jesus.*

I pray these stories of my struggles, setbacks, and even victories will inspire you to chase Jesus with every part of your being. I am praying for YOU, and I can't wait to hear how God whispers to you along this journey.

— Cassie

WRITING HIS-STORY

Staring out at the ocean, I can't help being in awe of the splendid masterpiece God painted so long ago. The strength and the force He drew within the tide. With each stroke of His hand, God painted strength and beauty right into every drop of water. God is truly a creator, a masterpiece maker, a story writer, and He craves to create something extraordinary with your life and mine.

In my private time with the Lord He carried this question to my mind, "how did I get here?" I stewed on and mulled over this question, seeking meaning to it, delving into the answer for a question I'm unsure I understand. So, how did I get here? Where is here? As I sought God's answers to these questions, He was faithful to shed some light and reveal to me what He means. He showed me all the incredible ways He's been moving in my life. *Here*, is the place I am in. *Here*, is my life. So how did I get here writing this devo, raising these kids, married to this man, serving in this church, publishing this book, speaking to those women, hosting that retreat?

It's been 16 years since I gave my life to Jesus and if I had to describe to someone what that looked like in one word, I would say journey. Following Jesus has been a journey and like every adventure, it's been full of difficulties and delights, high's and lows, good times and bad times.

This faith journey we are walking isn't one full of rainbows and butterflies, although I promise we will catch a glimpse of them along the way. Our faith journey is often full of tough choices, sacrifice, and being comfortable feeling uncomfortable. Following Jesus is usually a paradox. If you want to be strong, you must first become weak. You must serve to be served, and you must surrender to become blessed.

It's so easy for us to stand outside looking into someone's picture-perfect life and wish that were our story. But sister, this life isn't about our story, it's *His-story* and God longs to take our life and create something beautiful and unimaginable with it. He wants to paint you a masterpiece. You may look at some and see picture-perfect. Your neighbor seems to have Gods brush strokes all over her life. Financially she is doing well and all her kids teeth are straight. Daddy appears super involved, and mom is always baking new dishes. It's great that we see the beauty God is painting in others. But the book God writes with your life, with her life, will not always be simple. When God writes His-story, He does so with the knowledge of the future, a future we cannot see. I am where I am because with each mark of His pen or stroke of His brush I said, "yes Lord." And with each "yes Lord," has come a wrestling of the spirit, mind, and flesh. I have argued, wept, yelled, and all but given up on the things God's been writing in my life. There are things that you may never know about my journey to *here*. There are brush strokes in my painting that you will never see and words in my story you will never read, but they are there. They are part of my adventure, part of the story God is writing with my life.

I don't know what story He's writing for you, but I know this; it's a bestseller. The things God is lining up for you are extraordinary.

When I take a moment to look around and soak up the life God's writing for me, I'm in reverence of Him. I never imagined this is where I would be: writing this devo, mothering these kids, married to this man, publishing this book, speaking to these women, or serving in this church.

Friend, you may feel like your life is a mess, like it can never be beautiful, or like your life has no purpose. But praise God that He sees the beauty in the broken, a message in our mess, and He can take our history and turn in into *His-story*. No one's life is perfect, but when we let the author and finisher of our faith (Hebrews 12:2) write our story, life will have a perfect purpose, a perfect ending, and be full of wonderful miracles.

"God rewrote the text of my life when I opened the book of my heart to his eyes."

(PSALM 18:24 MSG)

Daily Prayer:

Lord, as I look around, I am in awe of you. You are so kind and so creative when painting the world. Just as you painted a masterpiece of the earth, I know you long to create a masterpiece with my life. Lord, paint my picture and write my pages just as you would have them to be. Write a bestseller with my life, paint a masterpiece. I realize I may not feel like my life involves much beauty, but I trust that when the book is complete, and the painting is a portrait, it will be the most magnificent work I've ever seen. You are good and so faithful. I thank you for choosing my life to create something incredible. I love you, Lord. Open my heart to your story for my life. Walk with me through these next 60 days. Keep me focused and pliable. Mold me and make me the woman you have made me to be. In Jesus name, Amen.

GIANTS, ARKS, AND LANGUAGE ARTS

I'm settled at my desk this morning captured by the gleaming wet leaves whirling in the breeze. If I didn't know any better, I'd swear it was ice glistening, but it's still August and very much summer-time outside. Either way, it's such a charming sight to my bleary eyes this morning. Last night wasn't the pleasant sleep I imagined it would be as I crept into bed. Instead, I laid wide awake watching 1, then 2, and on to 3 A.M. pass by on the clock. The struggle to sleep wasn't from a lack of exhaustion. We kicked off our school year yesterday, but the sleep struggle was because of a decision I would face just a few hours later.

You may not know this about me, but I am one of those crazy moms you hear about. You know: a homeschool mom. Our family loves home-school. I treasure having my children home with me, and they prefer having most Fridays off to chill out with their dad. The travel perks are nice too. Traveling back home to see our family without many missed days is awesome. Overall, it's wonderful. However, there is a minor battle with our youngest child's reading skills.

Tyler, my youngest, has dealt with this conflict in reading since kin-dergarten. I've done all I know to do, but year after year I feel like I've let him down. I realize you may think I should put him in school. And just to assure you, we are far from anti-public school. Dustin and I both graduated from public High School, and our children have spent 50% of their school careers in public school. Our choice to homeschool had zero to do with the school itself, and everything to do with what God spoke to us. Even when I don't understand what God is doing, I resolve to answer yes when He speaks.

Back to the decision I was dealing with. Because of Tyler's struggle with reading and my feeling of failure, I had reached out to the principal about enrolling him part-time for language classes. Administration was so friendly and happy to support us in any way they could. Tyler, however, wasn't super excited (because of early mornings, is my theory), but we made the plunge and headed off to the open house to meet his new part-time teacher. She was wonderful in every way, and he was ready to start his first day. That evening I arrived home, cooked dinner, watched a movie with the family, and climbed into bed. I never had another concern about my decision to enroll him part-time until my head reached the pillow. That's when the battle began.

Overwhelmed with sorrow because of our decision, I felt we had made the wrong choice. I cried out to God for answers, and He whispered to me, "Cassie, I have created Tyler to learn and understand and I have equipped you to teach him." Realizing once more, I had doubted what God could do in Tyler's life, and in my own. I had denied Him access to that part of my life.

Sometimes on this adventure called life, God will call us to things we don't understand, or things we don't feel prepared for. But, if we allow Him access, we can achieve all He has for us. No matter how you feel or how it appears, I invite you to say, "Yes, God."

Noah, the great ark builder (Genesis 6-9) was an ordinary guy with a monstrous task before him. David, the giant slayer (1 Samuel 17) was a shepherd lad, another ordinary guy that God equipped with a sling and a stone. I have no idea what you are facing, maybe there's an ark to build or a giant to kill in your life, but this is what I know. If God calls you, he equips you.

> *"May the God of peace who brought up from the dead our Lord Jesus, the great shepherd of the sheep, by the blood of the eternal covenant, equip you with everything good that you may do his will, working in us that which is pleasing in his sight, through Jesus Christ, to whom be glory forever and ever. Amen."*
>
> (HEBREWS 13:20-21 CSB)

Daily Prayer:

Father, thank you for equipping me long before I said "yes" to the assignment. I may face some big giants today, but you have equipped me with a bigger faith. Lord, may I not fall down in fear when confronted with hard times and laboring tasks, but help me lean into you and the equipping you are doing in me. God, I believe you can do anything you wish with my life and I ask you keep me humble and teachable. In Jesus name, Amen.

THIS IS ME

"The tongue has the power of life and death, and those who love it will eat its fruit."

(*PROVERBS 18:21 ESV*)

Why is it we only accept the one phrase that hurts? You can have a million words said to you, but only *receive* the one that hurts. Have you been there? Me too. Recently, I spent the evening pouring into a group of women when one of them tore me down. Crazy, right? One person's remarks can have such power over how we think and feel. I was hurt. Her comments were hurtful and discouraging. The silly part is, I had way more ladies offering me words of encouragement that evening. Yet, one hurtful remark, one discouraging observation is all I heard.

So, how do I receive everything else? How do I quit paying attention to what naysayers think? How do I become more like my husband, a professional naysayer combatant? He has the thickest skin of anybody I've ever met and the capability to love people despite how they wound him. Someday when I grow up, I want to be just like him. I'm joking about that, but, how do we avoid letting the unkind words and the naysayers take us down? How do we forbid every harsh remark from invading our core and taking it as the truth?

As I was whining to my hubs about the situation, he reminded me I don't need the approval of man. It matters how God looks at me. So right now, I'm choosing to be brave.

This is me.

My name is Cassie. I carry my heart on my sleeve and long for the love of others. I adore pajamas and get grumpy when I have to put on a bra or dress up. I get up way too early and am cranky by lunch (my kids can confirm this). Kayaking and on the beach make my heart whole. Mice, spiders, sharks and mountain lions terrify me; I often have nightmares of one or the other. I dream of all the ways I can lead women closer to Jesus. I imagine writing a best-selling book and purchasing a vacation home in Hawaii. My top priority in life is my faith, family and ministry.

I drink too much sweet tea, overeat pepperoni pizza, and consume way too many tacos. I hate veggies and I like very few fruits. I workout 7 minutes each day and despise every second. I love people passionately and thus, tend to become hurt easily. My family is far from perfect, but they are perfectly mine. I'm flipping proud of my kids and where I come from. I'm not embarrassed of my past, but embrace it and all that God can do with it.

Friend, this is me. This is who God designed me to be, and today I am embracing ME. I invite you: embrace you too! You can believe I'm crazy for dreaming so big, you're allowed your opinion. But no longer will I let anybody's opinion of me determine my worth. Sweet sister, neither should you.

"As you come to him, a living stone — rejected by people but chosen and honored by God "

(1 Peter 2:4 CSB)

Daily Prayer:

Lord, the scripture says there is power of life and death in the tongue, and I have met that first hand. People have sought to bring me down with their words and opinions of me, but today I declare life over me. Today, I accept that YOUR words have more power over my life than that of the cynics. Lord, thank you I can run to your word and discover all the precious words you express about me. You have called me loved, accepted, chosen, enough, and you have claimed me as your own. No longer will I let the hurtful comments of others penetrate my heart, but I will first pass them through the filter of Jesus. Thank you for sending your Son for me, so I can live the full life He came to give me. In Jesus name, Amen.

Leave it Lay

1 2 a.m… 3:20 a.m… 5 a.m… The darkness and my thoughts were surrounding me, suffocating me, and if I cried out to God once to please let me sleep, I asked Him a hundred times.

It's been challenging around my house lately to find space to be alone with Jesus. We had a pipe burst and flood half our home and nothing has been fun or easy about this process. In all honesty, it's been challenging to have normalcy around here, which includes my quiet time when I rest in Jesus and listen for His voice.

Over the past year and a half, I have been going through a season of wilderness. God is graciously leading me through the process, and I believe I'm on my way to the promise He has for me. However, along the way, I have experienced some isolation and even some rejection from others. The wilderness can often be a lonely place, and I have been battling this part of the process for months. Most days, I seem to have a handle on it, and then there're nights like last night.

I lay there, watching the hours pass by, and in the night's stillness, I broke. The thoughts of friendships falling apart, the fear of disappointing people and the fear that I am not enough haunted me. But amid the terror racing through my mind, I heard God whisper, ""Give. It. To. Me. You don't have to carry this. Let me take it from you." This whisper was an "aha" moment for me. I've laid this struggle down before, but somewhere along the way, I picked it back up. I'm carrying something I'm not meant to shoulder and all the while I'm convinced God forgot I gave to Him. The reality is, I took it back from Him.

As I lay there emptied of myself, I understood I may have to put this thing down a hundred times a day and that's okay. Laying in bed, one minute, I would have such peace in my surrender, only to have the fiery darts flying as I shut my eyes to rest. So once again, I placed it back down, gave God permission to take it back, and time after time, He happily received it back. And what I'm learning is, the more I hand it to Him, the less I want it back.

> *Now the Lord is the Spirit, and where the Spirit of the Lord is, there is freedom.*
>
> 2 CORINTHIANS 3:17

God wants us to rest in the freedom only He can give us. If you've felt like God has forgotten your burden, try giving it back to Him. If you do this a million times a day, don't let it discourage you. God came to set us free from all sin and all the things that enslave us. He's delighted to take it from you, however many times that may be.

Leave. It. Lay.

> *Out of my distress, I called on the Lord; The Lord answered me and set me free.*
>
> PSALM 118:5

Daily Prayer:

Jesus, this thing I'm carrying around with me is getting awfully heavy. Some days I feel like I may never be free of it but I know your shoulders are much larger than mine and you are ready and willing to carry it for me. Lord, give me strength today to hand it over and leave it lay. Extend the peace that surpasses all understanding, as I hand it to you. Jesus, I know I may pick this burden up a million times today, but give me the strength to lay it down a million and one. In Jesus name, Amen.

REMEMBER WHEN

January 15, 2011, should have altered the lives of my children, family, and friends forever. I won't go into all the details, but that's the night the Titanic went down (not the actual Titanic, but the nickname of the riverboat we were in). Me and my hubby, Dustin, were out that evening on our final gigging trip of the season with my dad and step momma. The four of us were enjoying our night when we started having boat trouble and shortly thereafter, struck a root-wad that drowned our ship (riverboat).

When the boat struck the icy root-wad, the strong current of the river pulled us from the boat. My stepmom became caught in the gigging rails of the boat, Dustin swept downstream, and yours truly trapped in a root-wad and submerged up to my collar in the frigid water. My dad was the only one to escape the current. None of us should have survived the night, but thankfully we did and I'm able to share this message with you today.

Reminded of that night, I realized January 15 had come and gone and this was my first thought about it this year. How can I overlook the night I almost died? I'm uncertain, but, it's possible. This thought has challenged me and so my challenge to you today is, remember when.

When I took the time to think back and remember, it caused me to see all God has done. Remembering when helped to establish in me a grateful heart. I glance back now and realize all I could've missed, and how different my family's lives could have been. Remembering when, I become thankful for the little things that too often I take for granted. However, when reflecting, I can look forward knowing God is more than capable to perform incredible, miraculous, and mighty works in my future.

In Joshua 4:1-24, God told Joshua to set up twelve stones on the other side of the Jordan River as a memorial. God didn't want the Israelites to forget what He had done. Like you and I, they needed these stones to remind them to share it with their children and the rest of the world.

I don't know your miracles, I only know mine. Perhaps you are reading this, and you struggle to see any miracles. Can I remind you, your salvation was a miracle? If nothing else, share the good news of salvation with someone. Perhaps you have an incredible story of how God pulled you out of drug addiction, or how He has healed your body or the body of someone you love. Share it! The world needs to learn about His goodness. The world needs reminded of how great our God is and so do we. If we wrestle with forgetting to be grateful for the big things, how can we ever remember and live with thanksgiving of the small stuff?

In our fast-paced living, it's easy to overlook or lose sight of what God has accomplished. Am I right? Sometimes I feel like people don't want to hear my story. I've shared it so many times already, but the Lord continues to nudge me because someone needs reminded of what He can do.

So let's agree, no longer will we allow the enemy to steal our story. We will share God's goodness and we'll remember what He's done and we will believe He is more than capable to perform the supernatural again and again!

But then I recall all you have done, O LORD; I remember your wonderful deeds of long ago.

(PSALM 77:11 CSB)

Daily Prayer:

Lord, thank you for causing me to recall all the beautiful and miraculous things you've accomplished in my life. Lord, help me never take those moments for granted or overlook your kindness. Give me the courage to share them with others and boldness to move them toward you. Lord, I choose to always remember. In Jesus name, Amen.

DAY SIX
———

OUR FUTURE

Like every September 11th, I sat remembering my first-hour math class, replaying the image of the planes hitting one building after another. Still, I recall the heartbreak and shock I felt watching people drop from the windows of the Twin Towers, as they had no other way out and the concern that rushed over me as a senior in high school about to enter the world that was being threatened before my very eyes. September 11th is a day that I will always remember. A day I take time to talk about each year with my children, still taking a moment to pray for the families who lost loved ones and praising God for the heroes of that day.

Like most years on September 11th, I listened to a speech delivered by President Trump from the fields of Shanksville, Pennsylvania- the crash site of United Airlines Flight 93. The stories he mentioned were tear jerkers. President Trump recounted story after story of loved one's calling their families from the airplane to declare "I love you" one last time. He told stories of miracles that only God himself could orchestrate, like how one wife had asked only for her husband's wedding ring from the wreckage. It seemed hopeless she would ever see it again as it was like hunting for a needle in a haystack, but this woman knew well the power of prayer. To her surprise, years later, greeted by a man at her front door, he held the wallet and the wedding band of her late husband (insert sobs).

President Trump spoke about a time when everyone, despite their color, race, or background, came together as a unified country, and one thing in particular he said took ahold of my heart.

"America's future is not written by our enemies."

— President Donald Trump

What a beautiful statement, full of truth and encouragement as we fight for our country and our freedom. But if I may, I'd like to replace our Presidents words with my own. I say to you, "your future is not written by the enemy."

I understand all too well how the enemy loves to convince us we ARE nothing, we'll DO nothing, GO nowhere, and that we have NO future. The enemy rejoices in causing us to dispute the goodness of God and the plans He has for us. But there is one thing he cannot do, and that is to rewrite our future! Satan has NO authority to rewrite what God has already written. Satan will try to convince us to doubt God and His plans. He whispers lies to us like, "we're not enough, and God can't use us." He'll urge us to look at what we have done, or where we have come from. Our adversary will tell us we're not smart enough or strong enough.

When we let the enemy inside our head, we doubt the future God has written for us.

Friend, let's not allow Satan to steal the future God has already written, the future that's waiting for us. We're God's creation, created by Him and for Him. He calls us worthy, enough, loved, accepted, child, and friend. I realize it's simple to speak these things and tougher to believe them. And if you're not convinced that He loves you and has a future for you, I encourage you to get into His word. All the truth you need is tucked away in its pages.

Your eyes saw me when I was formless; all my days were written in your book and planned before a single one of them began.

PSALM 139:16 (CSB)

Daily Prayer:

Father, today I choose your story for my life. Today I oppose any plan that the enemy has to draw my eyes off of you, what you have for my future, or who you say I am. May I not weaken when the adversary comes at me with his smooth little lies, but ready myself, embedded in YOUR word to fight back with the truth. Jesus, thank you for defeating the enemy long before I met him. Thank you for offering me the same power to fight as you carry inside of you. Lord, today I claim the future you have for me. In Jesus name, Amen.

THE NAME THAT CHANGES EVERYTHING

My daughter, Annah, became limp and seemingly lifeless in my trembling arms that cool, spring morning. She was 17 months old, and it looked as if she may not make it to her second birthday. This wasn't the first time we had a serious health scare with her. At three weeks old, she had contracted a dangerous case of RSV and spent seven days in Children's Hospital in St. Louis. As unnerving as it was to see her tiny, fragile body in the hospital then, this incident was more horrifying than then.

The night before "the incident", we were hosting our church youth group to several teenage girls and their leaders. That morning, I had about 15 girls in my home. Annah woke up, and my sister brought her to me because of her feeling feverish. Her body felt like she could start a fire. I gave her a dosage of Tylenol, and while doing so, I heard my husband and my dad pull into the driveway. As I took Annah to greet them at the door, her body went limp, her eyes rolled back into her head, and horror set in.

I yelled for a group leader, and she took Annah to determine if she could help. She thought Annah was experiencing a seizure and suggested I call an ambulance. As I called the ambulance, another woman called on

Jesus. When the seizure ended, Annah still laid unconscious and unable to respond. We loaded her up and headed the thirty plus miles to the ER. On the way to the hospital I realized this may be the last time I ever hold my baby girl. I began calling out to Jesus. I didn't know what to say, but I knew *that* name could save my little girl. And if she didn't make it, I knew *that* name would comfort me.

Thankfully Annah made a full recovery, but there have been many times in my life that I didn't know what to pray or how to pray. So I do what I know and call out to Jesus. The name of Jesus is the only name that brings life amid death, saves the lost, and restores marriages, friendships, and relationships. It is the name that heals. It is the name that changes *everything*.

In Mark 10, we are told of a man who also called out to Jesus in his time of need:

> *"They came to Jericho. And as He was leaving Jericho with His disciples and a large crowd, Bartimaeus (the son of Timaeus), a blind beggar, was sitting by the road. When he heard that it was Jesus the Nazarene, he began to cry out, "Son of David, Jesus, have mercy on me!" Many people told him to keep quiet, but he was crying out all the more, "Have mercy on me, Son of David!" Jesus stopped and said, "Call him." So they called the blind man and said to him, "Have courage! Get up; He's calling for you." He threw off his coat, jumped up, and came to Jesus. Then Jesus answered him, "What do you want Me to do for you?" "Rabbouni," the blind man told Him, "I want to see!" "Go your way," Jesus told him. "Your faith has healed you." Immediately he could see and began to follow Him on the road."*
>
> MARK 10:46-52 CSB

I understand this story happened centuries ago, but even though times have changed, Jesus has not. He promises to never leave us or forsake us. The name of Jesus is as powerful in your situation now as it was for blind Bartimaeus back then. Sometimes you may not know what to pray, but the name of Jesus is enough. The life of blind Bartimaeus forever changed because of one name. *Jesus.*

Are you are dealing with a situation, and you don't know what to do? Call out to Jesus! Have you been living life your way, and it just isn't working? Call out to Jesus! The name of Jesus has the power to save you from whatever keeps you bound. When life gets hard, and you can't imagine a way out, call out all the louder, and don't allow Him to pass you by. His name changes *everything.*

Daily Prayer:

Jesus, Jesus. The name above every name. Lord, as I face trials in my life, and go through struggles, I call out all the louder. Jesus, I desire you to stand in the middle of my situations, I need you to stand in the middle of my life today. I desire you and the power you bring to transform everything. God, thank you for sending Jesus to me. Thank you for the fullness of life He brings. In Jesus name, Amen.

CHASE GRACE

D o you ever find yourself overwhelmed? It seems as if there's plenty of striving, working, and chasing to do. Sometimes we're over-whelmed by trying to earn our way to the top of the corporate ladder or earn the love of a friend. You know that vicious cycle of working to be enough for this or that? Me too. This struggle of striving is one of my biggest challenges, and far too often. I'm a go-getter by nature, and I don't believe it's a bad quality to have; it can be great. However, if misused, this quality God gave me can have adverse effects. The positive side is that when God gives me a vision, I take off doing all I can to make it hap-pen. Maybe you've heard the saying, "pray as it depends on God, work as it depends on you". I have the work part down, but the trouble is, my work mentality spills over into my relationship with Jesus. I do things to earn God's grace, and He's left out, it becomes about me. Friend, we need not try and earn something that God says is free. Let's be real, sister. We wouldn't walk into our favorite retail store with a gift card and demand we pay for our clothes. Am I right!?

Maybe you relate. You're also a doer, and it's been a blessing when it's a promotion at work or chasing what feels like 13 kids around all day. Perhaps you can relate as you lead a small group each week. DOING isn't wrong unless we make grace about what we do instead of what Jesus did.

In Luke 18, Jesus tells us that rather than doing more, we are to let go of everything and follow him. Growing up, my parents taught to be a good girl—a rule follower and I believe that's sound advice: We as Christ followers need to live in such a way that illuminates Jesus in our life. Instead of doing more or always striving to be better, Jesus calls us to sacrifice, to let go, and follow Him.

> *One day one of the local officials asked him, "Good Teacher, what must I do to deserve eternal life?" Jesus said, "Why are you calling me good? No one is good - only God. You know the commandments, don't you? No illicit sex, no killing, no stealing, no lying, honor your father and mother." He said, "I've kept them all for as long as I can remember." When Jesus heard that, he said, "Then there's only one thing left to do: Sell everything you own and give it away to the poor. You will have riches in heaven. Then come, follow me." This was the last thing the official expected to hear. He was very rich, and the Word says he became sad. He was holding on tight to a lot of things and not about to let them go. Seeing his reaction, Jesus said, "Do you have any idea how difficult it is for people who have it all to enter God's kingdom? I'd say it's easier to thread a camel through a needle's eye than get a rich person into God's kingdom." "Then who has any chance at all?" the others asked. "No chance at all," Jesus said, "if you think you can pull it off by yourself. Every chance in the world if you trust God to do it." Peter tried to regain some initiative: "We left everything we owned and followed you, didn't we?" "Yes," said Jesus, "and you won't regret it. No one who has sacrificed home, spouse, brothers and sisters, parents, children - whatever - will lose out. It will all come back multiplied many times over in your lifetime. And then the bonus of eternal life!"*
>
> LUKE 18:18-30 (MSG)

From the first sentence, the official had it all wrong. He asked, "What must *I* do?" This rich man had the same mindset you and I often carry around, "What can *I* do, Lord, to earn the grace and eternal life *you* offer?"

This man being a Pharisee was likely raised to follow the rules, the laws. Jesus being all-knowing was aware the man would likely answer saying he had kept the commandments. Jesus goes ahead and names a few to get it out of the way and moves on to the real issue: letting go. The rich man was doing everything right, but in his striving, it caused some self-righteousness to well up inside of him. The rich man became too dependent upon himself and his wealth. Jesus recognized this, and He tells the man, "Sell all you have and follow me." Let go of it all, stop striving and working, and follow me. Stop allowing the chase to steal your joy and follow me. Pursue me. Chase grace. But the man couldn't do it. He couldn't stop *doing*, and he went away sad. The rich man wasn't willing to surrender everything to Christ. He wouldn't let go of what he had to gain the grace Christ could give.

When we depend on self, we wind up overwhelmed and sad. You may even know the effects of depression and hopelessness. On our own, we can never be all we need to be. We must let go of what we have so we can enjoy what only Christ can give. Jesus is the only way to joy and peace in this crazy life. Without Jesus, we will end up exhausted, sad, discouraged, and angry. This is my encouragement for you today: let go of the striving and chase grace.

Then he said to them all, "If anyone wants to follow after me, let him deny himself, take up his cross daily, and follow me.

(LUKE 9:23 CSB)

Daily Prayer:

Lord, today in my striving to do good things, or be better, earn promotions, and earn favor, may I remember you. Help me understand life apart from you is hard. Your grace and love make life joyful and pleasant. Jesus, help me fix my eyes on you and the free grace you offer. Help me say "no" to striving today and say "yes" to the grace you stand ready to extend. In Jesus name, Amen.

DAY NINE

BELIEVE IN ME

"Believe in me," God whispered as I rested at the pond with the sounds of nothing but the breeze, water ripples, and an occasional croaking frog. I often go to the pond to think, write, and be alone with God. It's my little sanctuary, right here at home. I had been sick all week and had spent limited time with God other than begging him to heal me and my kiddos. I yearned to be with Him and hear from Him that day at the pond. It seemed like an eternity since I had heard His voice or spent much time with Him.

Now, to be honest, the words "believe in me," shocked me. I believe in God, not only do I believe in Him, I devote my life trying to follow Him and encourage others to do the same. What did He mean, "believe in me?"

As I sat there puzzled by what He said, I heard the Holy Spirit explain. While I believe in Him, I sometimes struggle to believe what He wants do through me. I believe He can heal my loved ones and believe He can take my friend's music ministry to the next level. I know the Lord can do crazy, amazing things in the lives of my pastors, but I wrestle to believe He will do what He says He will do in my life. There are times I get excited about what He's spoken to me, only to water it down, making it easier to believe in my little mind. I have seen God do wonderful things in my life that only He could do, yet I still doubt He can do it again.

Today I'm reminded of Joshua. Joshua had seen God work around him and through him time after time, but I wonder if while marching around the walls of Jericho, day after day, if he questioned that God could do it again?

As God pointed me to Joshua's story, I recognized his obedience to every word God spoke. Joshua's obedience to what God said made way for God to use Him. Maybe you're wondering if the walls will fall or if God is willing and able to do it again. The answer is: YES! Stop *doubting* and start *believing* that God is ready and able to do crazy, amazing things in your life, believe and obey.

> *"On the seventh day they rose early, at the dawn of day, and marched around the city in the same manner seven times. It was only on that day that they marched around the city seven times. And at the seventh time, when the priests had blown the trumpets, Joshua said to the people, "Shout, for the Lord has given you the city."*
>
> (JOSHUA 6:15-16 CSB)

Daily Prayer:

Lord, I believe you are who you say you are and that you will do what you say you will do. I put my trust in you and in all of your ways. I may not understand everything I go through on my way around the walls, but I trust you have my best interest at heart. Lord, help my belief to stand firm in the trials. Thank you, that you have far more significant things for me than my mind can imagine. I wait patiently, Lord. In Jesus name, Amen.

DAY TEN

IDENTITY THEFT

In a world full of technology, credit and debit cards, online applications, smartphones, and greedy, jealous, and deceitful people, identity theft is an *extreme* issue. People are stealing our identities to make a few extra dollars or using our FICO score to score for themselves the latest gadget or pickup truck (the truck you've dreamed of that they now own thanks to your information). It's a real epidemic in our country and the crazy thing is, it's nearly impossible to find the thieves hiding behind your identity. A stolen and damaged identity is a lengthy process to recover.

While it's common to have our personal identity threatened, it's twice as common to have our spiritual identity threatened. I would say it's threatened daily. For some of us, it's a moment by moment battle. The upside to all of this is we're not the only ones who wrestle with it.

Adam and Eve were the first people, and the first to have their spiritual identity stolen. The sneaky serpent comes along and offers his sweet little lies and before you know it, out of their shame, Adam and Eve are hiding from God, the same God they walked with shamelessly before. They bought the lie, and their identity in God is robbed from them (Genesis 3). Then, we have Jacob and Esau. Jacob, jealous of Esau, who was their father's favorite, lied to his vulnerable father and stole Esau's identity. But it wasn't just his identity Jacob wanted. It was what Esau's identity stood for; blessing (Genesis 27).

From the very beginning, identity theft has been an issue. People are robbing others of their identity and Satan is whispering his lies and watching as we buy into every word. Often never stopping to consider the whispers we hear and we need to ask: whose words we are buying?

A few months ago, I heard Christine Caine speak at an Outcry Worship event, and something she said made its way into my Evernote App. She said, "If you want to know the lies of the enemy, you must apply the truth of God's Word."

How elementary, yet powerful, that thought is. We get whispered many lies that have the very purpose of snatching our identity, and instead of comparing them to God's Word about us, we compare them to our version of us. From where we stand, they feel right, so they must be true. Someone has called you a failure. It might feel accurate, but God says you will prevail. Satan whispers, "worthless," but God says "worthy."

You see how this works? The lies will come but we have to illuminate them with God's Word. If I refuse to pass the whispers through my God filter, my identity becomes jeopardized. Before long, my identity is no longer found in Christ, but in a lie. And just like the long, laboring process of identity theft recovery, we have to start over. We have to train our thoughts to be the thoughts of Christ; we have to *rebuild* our identity.

Friend, I invite you to filter the words, whether they come from others or the enemy, filter them through God's Word. God's Word will illuminate *every* lie. I once heard my pastor say, "Whatever Satan says, believe the opposite." Satan says you'll never make it, but the truth is God is making a way. Satan says you're not loved, but God sent His son because He loved you *so* much!

I am praying for you, friend. You are not alone on this journey, open your Bible and dig into what God reveals about you. It's like having your very own identity theft protection coverage, absolutely free!

"So Jesus said to the Jews who had believed him, "If you abide in my word, you are truly my disciples, and you will know the truth, and the truth will set you free."

(JOHN 8:31-32 CSB)

Daily Prayer:

Lord, today I ask for your identity protection. Point me to the truth that is your word. Show me who YOU see and who YOU have created me to be. Don't allow the naysayers of my life to rob me of my identity in you. Give me boldness to be the person YOU have formed me to be. No longer will I let the adversary or others tell me who I am. Lord, I praise you for your Word that is the truth. In Jesus name. Amen.

BARTERING FOR A BLESSING

I have a friend who, in college, used to barter his food. We spent countless hours over two years laughing at his approach to getting a decent meal. Most of his meals comprised peanut butter, bananas and the occasional splurge on dino bites. My husband and I did our best to make sure we were feeding him well while he was home, and I know his momma did the same. One year to help him out, we had a small, going back-to-college get together for him and asked people to bring him some of his favorite foods. We figured he'd eat it or barter it for something that sounded more appetizing. My hubs and I didn't care, we just hoped to keep him alive. On Halloween after a weenie roast, we sent him packing with hotdogs and buns. To no one's surprise, he chose not to eat them, but he could trade them for something tastier. His bartering stories always kept us laughing and kept him eating.

While reading through the book of Judges, I came across the story of Jephthah, and God planted this thought of "bartering for a blessing" inside me. Like our friend swapping his food, I believe on occasion we are guilty of bartering for blessings with the Lord.

"Lord, if you will do this, then I'll do this." Have you ever prayed this prayer? Or one similar? I've had my fair share of prayers like this. It has taken time and lots of spiritual growth for me to learn that there is no bartering with the Lord. God wants to bless us, but He doesn't need you to make deals with him. He needs you to be obedient. Blessings will always hinge on our obedience to Him.

Back to Jephthah. He was in a pickle and needed God to protect him and choose him and the Israelites over the Ammonites.

29 The Spirit of the Lord came on Jephthah, who traveled through Gilead and Manasseh, and then through Mizpah of Gilead. He crossed over to the Ammonites from Mizpah of Gilead. 30 Jephthah made this vow to the Lord: "If you in fact hand over the Ammonites to me, 31 whoever comes out the doors of my house to greet me when I return safely from the Ammonites will belong to the Lord, and I will offer that person as a burnt offering."

(JUDGES 11:29-31 CSB)

We need to pause here for a moment. I need to point out that in verse 29, the spirit of the Lord came on Jephthah, but in verse thirty he makes a deal with the Lord. God was already with him, but Jephthah, not convinced, made a deal with God.

32 Jephthah crossed over to the Ammonites to fight against them, and the Lord handed them over to him. 33 He defeated twenty of their cities with a great slaughter from Aroer all the way to the entrance of Minnith and to Abel-keramim. So the Ammonites were subdued before the Israelites.

(JUDGES 11:32-33 CSB)

WHOOP WHOOP! Insert happy dance. It's okay, no one's watching. The Lord did just as He promised and defeated the Ammonites. Jephthah had to be on cloud nine that God held up His end of the deal. I can only imagine what his victory dance may have looked like. There was one problem, as excited and victorious as he may have felt, Jephthah still had to hold up his end of the deal.

34 When Jephthah went to his home in Mizpah, there was his daughter, coming out to meet him with tambourines and dancing! She was his only child; he had no other son or daughter besides her. 35 When he saw her, he tore his clothes and said, "No! Not my daughter! You have devastated me! You have brought great misery on me. I have given my word to the Lord and cannot take it back."

(JUDGES 11:34-35 CSB)

Wait. What?! His daughter? What devastation he must have suffered? He went from feeling victorious to total ruin the moment she stepped through the doors to greet him. When I first read this, I thought, "Lord, why?" "Why would you require such a thing of him?" Then I remembered verse 29. The Lord came on Jephthah before he ever made a deal with God. God never required such a sacrifice from him, it's just the deal Jephthah made (v.31).

Too often, we're guilty of this very thing. We make deals with the Lord that we can never keep, and He would never require. Then we end up angry with Him when it's time to hold up our end. Why do we resist the truth that God wants to do great things for us? What if, instead of focusing on what we can do, we focus on what God wants to do, can do, and will do? How about we fix our focus on being obedient to His voice, His will, and His way? It is then and only then, that the blessings will flow. No bartering required unless you're trading hotdogs for a sirloin steak.

Then Samuel said: Does the Lord take pleasure in burnt offerings and sacrifices as much as in obeying the Lord? Look: to obey is better than sacrifice, to pay attention is better than the fat of rams.

(1 SAMUEL 15:22 CSB)

Daily Prayer:

Father, forgive me for my lack of trust. I sometimes struggle to let you work in your way and in your time. For this I am sorry. Help me be quick to listen to you and slow to speak. Give me opportunities to be obedient and to learn your voice. Lord, thank you for the grace you offer when I try to do things my way. In Jesus name, Amen.

Don't Forget to Breathe

S norkeling and I have a love-hate relationship. I love to snorkel, but I'm awful at it. Everything in me goes haywire when I strap fins to my feet and a mask to my face. It is a miracle I haven't encountered a hungry shark who's confused me with injured prey. I flop around like a busted up dolphin just trying to make my fins work.

A couple years ago, on vacation, I kicked my feet the wrong way for so long it caused shin splints. It's okay to chuckle; I'm laughing too! The fins are a nightmare for me, and the mask is the worst part. The issue is, when I attach the snorkel and the mask, I forget to breathe. I legit will hold my breath the whole time I snorkel. And yes, I realize that's what a snorkel is for, but the moment I put on the snorkel gear: GAME OVER.

I'm sure your way cooler than me and snorkeling isn't a problem for you, but what about in life? Do you ever struggle to breathe through everyday life? Life has a way of making us feel suffocated. Am I right? Maybe you've found yourself in a financial bind, and it's overwhelming, or you're a new member of the empty nesters club, and you're trying to catch your breath. You may wonder, "how in the world did this happen so fast?" (Speaking of, as a parent of teenagers, I'd love your tips on how to slow down time). Perhaps it's a diagnosis, and it's taken your breath. Maybe you're dealing with a rebellious child, and about the time you catch your breath, BAM! Another blow. For me, it seems like I have so much going on day to day, I just forget to *breathe*. Mundane becomes my mask.

Do you know what I find interesting? That I panic and hold my breath when I put on my mask, but the goggles themselves have nothing to do with my breathing. The goggles are there to keep water out. So why panic? All I need to do is attach the cute little snorkel and I can breathe.

For a snorkel set to work, you must connect the snorkel.

In life, this is the Holy Spirit, the Lord Himself. Life will come at you because that's what life does, there is no way around it. But, as followers of Jesus, we have the tool we need to keep breathing. He has given us the snorkel. Even when we feel surrounded on every side and it looks like, we may drown. We can breathe. I believe this is no new news to most of us. We have Jesus, and we see Him in our life. However, like me forgetting to breathe through the snorkel, we forget to use the ONE we have. Because Jesus lives *IN* us doesn't mean we are allowing Him to work *THROUGH* us.

What is keeping you from letting God take control of your situation? God gave us the tool we need, so why not use it?

The Holy Spirit is dwelling inside of you ready and eager to be whatever you need. Do you need peace? He is peace. Do you need comfort? He is comfort. How about some direction? He's that too. Holy Spirit is *what* you need *when* you need it.

> *"Peace I leave with you. My peace I give to you. I do not give to you as the world gives. Don't let your heart be troubled or fearful. You have heard me tell you, 'I am going away, and I am coming to you.'"*
> *(JOHN 14:27-28A CSB)*

Daily Prayer:

Father, today I CHOOSE you. I activate you in my life, to let you rule my situation. If I get bad news today, I will keep breathing through you. God, I understand sometimes life happens, and it hurts, but I trust you to bring about good in every bad situation. I will not allow my situation to dictate my breathing. I keep breathing because you, Lord, are my snorkel. In Jesus name. Amen.

THIS, IS EASY

I sat whining to my gracious mother on the other end of the phone. It had been a super sad day for me in all areas of "adulting." I'm sure I grumbled about anything I could think of as she kindly encouraged me, likely hoping we'd get disconnected and she could have her day back. Okay, that's not true, but I'm very thankful for a momma who listens and encourages me even if she may need the encouragement herself. As we hung up, I laughed and made a comment, "I'll gripe at ya later!" I well knew that was pretty much all I had done.

As my day went on, the discouragement I felt lingered until that evening. After dinner, I sat down on the couch with my journal and Bible *knowing* I needed to dig in, frustrated and disappointed with how things were going, doing anything else sounded better. The dream God had given me was not playing out the way *I* expected it to. It had been a year since He whispered the "idea" to me and I thought there would be some real progress by now. But I felt stuck and struggled to see the dream.

So there I sat, Bible and journal in hand. They were begging me to open them. Eventually, I gave in, knowing if I would just seek God, I'd find some encouragement. I started by venting to my journal like I had my poor momma. Much like my momma, my journal never seems to mind. To my surprise, as I poured myself out before the Lord, He listened.

I often wonder how long it will take before I understand and believe He wants to help me, encourage me, rescue me, and love me through these things. I'm always so surprised that He cares so much although He's never given me a reason to believe otherwise. Crazy, right? There I was, emptied of myself and praying for a word of encouragement as I opened my Bible. And there it was, tucked just a few short verses into my reading, I found the reassurance I needed. I found this gentle reminder from the Lord:

"This is easy in the Lord's sight."

(2 KINGS 3:18A CSB)

The Lord heard my cry, and He saw my struggle. My battle to believe He is capable of delivering on His word to me. From where I sit, it appears He's forgotten about me and the dream He gave me. He understands that the task at hand seems impossible. He understands my fear of lack in the situation and He reminds me that what I'm facing, well, it's easy for Him. It may not look accessible from where I sit, but it's nothing that one word from His mouth can't accomplish.

I may never know what discouragement or disappointments you may be facing. Perhaps it's discouragement in your health, finances, relationships, or maybe you too are staring at a "fading" dream, hopeless for God to revive it and revive you. Whatever it is you're facing, know that THIS is easy in the Lord's sight and He won't let you down.

Daily Prayer:

Father, thank you for seeing what I can't and that you've ALREADY prepared a way for me. Thank you I can trust you with my life and for having a divine purpose and direction for me. Lord, help me remain focused on you, rather than the storm I may be facing. The storm is often scary, but I'm grateful that you are bigger and stronger. Uphold me with your mighty right-hand today. In Jesus name. Amen.

PRESSING AND THRESHING

I'd like to tell on myself a bit. Do you mind?

I have always struggled with being sassy with my words and to make it worse, I'm also short-fused. Hard to believe? Maybe, but it's the truth. My Grandpa even blessed me with the nickname "Sassy" and goodness, did that stick like glue with the fam. You can see this has been a lifelong difficulty. I try to blame it on the fact that I have a sassy momma and a short-fused father, making me a time-bomb waiting to blow. The truth is, no one person or lame excuse has ever forced me to respond negatively in situations. That's ALL me! However, in my defense, over many years I'm learning how to control my attitude. Sometimes I need to walk away from a situation to cool off, but I am learning how and when to respond to things. I haven't mastered it yet, but I'm better than I once was.

Recently, while helping a friend with a work project, I dealt with some angry people who would yell at me over contracts and anything else they could think of. None of these people knew me, but they sure thought they could treat me like a criminal. How dare I do my job! Girl! Being yelled at was a hard pill to swallow for this sassy girl. I wanted to give them a good word thrashing and maybe a throat punch for good measure, but instead, I walked away.

As God spoke to me about this thought of pressing and threshing, it challenged me. I felt the Lord asking me, "Cassie, when you experience pressing and crushing, what oozes out of you?"

OUCH! Tough question. But do I dare ask you the same question? In the pressing and threshing of life, when people and things come against you and life gets hard, what oozes from you? Is it Jesus that seeps from your heart? Or is it anger, resentment, hatred, depression, anxiety or a host of other negative responses? When someone cuts you off in traffic, how do you respond? What about when the girls have a get-together, and you didn't get the invitation, do you express how much you'd love to join them next time or do you allow resentment to settle deep within you? When you feel picked over and undervalued at work or in ministry, how do you respond? When finances are overwhelming, family issues are on the rise, or when you are waiting on a miracle, what seeps out of you? Joy and Jesus? Fear and doubt? In my situation, I could have lashed out, but in doing so I forfeit the glory Jesus deserves.

To help you better understand the reference to pressing and threshing, I'm referring to making wine and grain in Bible days. When making wine, the people would stomp the grapes with their feet, causing the juices to flow from them (hopefully with clean feet unless you enjoy a little toe jam with your wine). To produce grain, they would take wheat and throw it onto the floor, allowing oxen and cattle to tread repeatedly over them. This process loosened the edible part of the cereal grain (or other crops) from the scaly, inedible chaff that surrounds it. Then winnowing forks were used to throw the mixture into the air so the wind could blow away the chaff, leaving only the good grain on the floor. It's the threshing and crushing that separated the edible from the inedible. But we get to *choose* what will ooze from us when we're pressed.

I want to be a woman who responds in such a way that God can use me and Jesus is glorified through me. I never want someone to question the Jesus in me because I oozed anger when pressed. Now, I'm not so naïve to think I will never struggle with responding the way Jesus would. My name isn't "Sassy Cassie" for nothing! I can, however, promise you this, I will spend my life trying to react with the love of Christ. Will you?

"This is my commandment, that you love one another as I have loved you."

(JOHN 15:12 CSB)

Daily Prayer:

Father, I know that the pressing is inevitable. I will face days that test me and my response, but Lord, more than anything, I want to respond like you. I want to show people what you look like, so Father, help me. The times of pressing aren't fun, but I am grateful for the opportunities to grow from them. Each time I am pressed and respond like you, I begin to look like you. Thank you for opportunities to look more like you. In Jesus name. Amen.

IT IS WELL

You may relate, but there are times that I struggle to keep the faith. Faith like that of the Shunammite woman. Have you heard her story? Let's look.

"One day Elisha went to Shunem. A prominent woman who lived there persuaded him to eat some food. So whenever he passed by, he stopped there to eat. Then she said to her husband, "I know that the one who often passes by here is a holy man of God, so let's make a small, walled-in upper room and put a bed, a table, a chair, and a lamp there for him. Whenever he comes, he can stay there."

One day he came there and stopped at the upstairs room to lie down. He ordered his attendant Gehazi, "Call this Shunammite woman." So he called her, and she stood before him. Then he said to Gehazi, "Say to her, 'Look, you've gone to all this trouble for us. What can we do for you? Can we speak on your behalf to the king or to the commander of the army?'" She answered, "I am living among my own people." So he asked, "Then what should be done for her?" Gehazi answered, "Well, she has no son, and her husband is old."

"Call her," Elisha said. So Gehazi called her, and she stood in

the doorway. Elisha said, "At this time next year you will have a son in your arms." Then she said, "No, my Lord. Man of God, do not lie to your servant." The woman conceived and gave birth to a son at the same time the following year, as Elisha had promised her. The child grew, and one day went out to his father and the harvesters. Suddenly he complained to his father, "My head! My head!" His father told his servant, "Carry him to his mother."

So he picked him up and took him to his mother. The child sat on her lap until noon and then died. She went up and laid him on the bed of the man of God, shut him in, and left. She summoned her husband and said, "Please send me one of the servants and one of the donkeys, so I can hurry to the man of God and come back again." But he said, "Why go to him today? It's not a New Moon or a Sabbath."

She replied, "Everything is alright." Then she saddled the donkey and said to her servant, "Go fast; don't slow the pace for me unless I tell you." So she came to the man of God at Mount Carmel.

When the man of God saw her at a distance, he said to his attendant Gehazi, "Look, there's the Shunammite woman. Run out to meet her and ask, 'Are you all right? Is your husband all right? Is your son all right?'" And she answered, "Everything's alright." When she came up to the man of God at the mountain, she clung to his feet. Gehazi came to push her away, but the man of God said, "Leave her alone—she is in severe anguish, and the Lord has hidden it from me. He hasn't told me."

Then she said, "Did I ask my Lord for a son? Didn't I say, 'Do not lie to me?'"

So Elisha said to Gehazi, "Tuck your mantle under your belt, take my staff with you, and go. If you meet anyone, don't stop to greet him, and if a man greets you, don't answer him. Then place my staff on the boy's face." The boy's mother said to Elisha, "As the Lord lives and as you yourself live, I will not leave you."

So he got up and followed her. Gehazi went ahead of them and *placed the staff on the boy's face, but there was no sound or sign of life, so he went back to meet Elisha and told him, "The boy didn't wake up."*

When Elisha got to the house, he discovered the boy lying dead on his bed. So he went in, closed the door behind the two of them, and prayed to the Lord. Then he went up and lay on the boy: he put mouth to mouth, eye to eye, hand to hand. While he bent down over him, the boy's flesh became warm. Elisha got up, went into the house, and paced back and forth. Then he went up and bent down over him again. The boy sneezed seven times and opened his eyes.

(2 KING 4: 8-35 CSB)

In verse seventeen God promised the woman a son which she gave birth to a year later. Years go by, and she watches her promise grow. Life was good until one day it wasn't. The boy fell ill, and not just sick, but the Bible says, "he died." What a blow that must have been. Her promise from the Lord was dead. The promise she had prayed for and cared for, the promise God didn't have to give her but chose to give her.

Can you relate? Perhaps you've not lost a child, but you've lost a dream. You've heard the voice of God, stepped out in faith, only to find your dream looking lifeless? John 16:33 reminds us that in this life, we *will* have trouble. Sometimes life throws us surprises, and not the good kind. It could be a diagnosis, a financial struggle, a rebellious child, marriage issues, or a host of other things. No matter what problem has wedged its way between you and your promise, don't start mourning just yet. It may not be as lifeless as it looks.

If you read on down, about verse 23, the Bible says, while the Shunammite woman's son lay dead, she goes on her way, saying, "it will be well." Call me crazy, but it doesn't seem too well to me. Her son is dead. It's over, let the tears flow! Nope. Not this momma. She responded with faith in the Promise-Giver. Momma was looking past her circumstances and straight at her promise. I hate to admit this to you, but too often I respond the opposite. I put more faith in my circumstances than I do in

God's promises. But I am learning that the way we react to our situations is often the very thing that determines whether our promise lives or dies. Had the Shunammite momma mourned her loss and never went to the man of God, her promise most likely would've died and stayed that way. There was no one else with the power to bring her son to life. And friend, there is no one besides God that has the power to revive your promise.

My question for you is this: how are you responding? Where have you put your faith? In your circumstances or in the promise-giver? God wants to breathe life back into your promise, despite how things appear. God will always accomplish what He says He will.

> "So my word that comes from my mouth will not return to me empty, but it will accomplish what I please and will prosper in what I send it to do."
>
> ISAIAH 55:11 (CSB)

Daily Prayer:

> Father, today I'm tired. I'm tired of the circumstances that lie to me and distract me from the promise you have for me. Lord, today I am choosing to trust your word over my life and over my situations. I know that not one word from your mouth will return void. Although things may LOOK lifeless, I am confident you can bring them to life again. Lord, I love you, and I wait for your promise. In Jesus name. Amen.

DAY SIXTEEN

No "Plan B"

D o you have a bible hero? Someone from scripture whose story you relate well with or whose story gives you a giant boost of encouragement each time you read about them? For me, that's the story of King David. I have read and re-read his story probably a hundred times if not more, but something seemingly new jumped out at me. It was like God tucked this little nugget away and is only now revealing it to me. I love how God works. I love how He knows just what we need, right when we need it.

> "David took Goliath's head and brought it to Jerusalem, but he put Goliath's weapons in his own tent."
>
> (1 SAMUEL 17:54 CSB)

Here's the little nugget I noticed: David had defeated the giant Goliath with a sling and a stone but decided he'd better chop his head off for good measure. When he finished taking care of Goliath, he brought his head to Jerusalem, but verse fifty-four states that he put Goliath's weapons in his own tent.

This scripture caught my attention. And I wondered, why? Why did David need Goliath's weapons? He had fought a giant and won with nothing more than a sling and a stone. Why keep his weaponry? I believe God is showing us that Goliath's weapons were provision for what would lay ahead of him. God knew he would need the weapons again, but this time, to fight mentally. To remind himself of what God had done before. When he looked at Goliath's weapons, it reminded him that God was bigger than any giant and more significant than their weapons. It reminded David he could defeat the most excellent defenses with greater faith. Those weapons would give him the courage to fight all the giants in his life. The biggest giant of all being King Saul. God needed David to remember, to never doubt, what God could do when he fought by faith.

I'm not sure when it happened, but the weapons ended up in the town of Nob, where David visits with a priest named Ahimelech. David told him he was on an urgent mission from the king and needed bread and a weapon. The priest told him, *"The sword of Goliath the Philistine, whom you killed in the valley of Elah, is here, wrapped in a cloth behind the ephod. If you want to take it for yourself, then take it."* (1 Samuel 21:9 CSB).

I wonder if when David heard what weapon was available, it caused him to remember God's greatness and if it increased his faith. God had always been with David and was with him now.

I also find it interesting that the sword was placed behind the ephod (a sleeveless garment worn by Jewish priests). While David may have felt the need to find protection from Saul, the ephod may have reminded him of his faith in God; our high priest was going before him and would fight this battle too. No sword needed, only David's trust in God to fight for him!

I understand all too well the need to grab my weapons and head out ready to fight my battles. I believe there is a time for us to take up arms, but more often than not, we get ahead of God, and fight battles He intends to fight for us. Sister, our faith in Jesus should always be our plan "A," not our plan "B".

Today I challenge you to think back for a moment and remind yourself of what God has done for you, the battles he's won for you, and the giants in your life that lay headless. Remember that if he did it then, He can do it again.

Daily Prayer:

Jesus, thank you for going ahead of me. Thank you for fighting my battles. There are days I wonder how I will ever make it through this fight, but then I am reminded of all the times you've fought for me and won. May I never lose sight of the past battles as they are preparing me for the future ones. Lord, teach me to wait on you when giants stand in my way. I am not meant to go ahead of you. You are the ONE who goes before me. In Jesus name. Amen.

ISLAND TIME

During my first trip to Maui in 2016, my husband and I quickly learned that when in Maui you're on island time, whether you want to be or not. The speed limits alone were enough to send us cliff diving. No matter where you were on the island, the speed limits were, at most, a whopping 45 mph. Now for folks like us who live our lives always running and rushing around, island time was hard for us to get used to. Eventually, it grew on us, and we hated to leave the change of pace when it was time to say, "Aloha." I expected we'd head back home and return to our crazy pace of life and I was right. Truth is, we are in a busy season of life. We do our best to manage it well, but it's hectic. Island time isn't realistic for us right now. But while island time may not be realistic in my every-day life, it is something God began stirring in me about my spiritual life. Particularly about His timing.

Often when God whispers to us, shows us things, or works in us, we assume He means today, and that isn't always the case. It seems like if He doesn't do what He says, when *we* think He should, we question if we heard Him correctly or we threaten to give up. Now you're the only one who can know for sure what God's speaking to you, but I encourage you not to throw the towel in just yet. I recently went through a rough season, and it's hard not to question His voice or doubt what He speaks to you. I'm here to tell you, He can and He will!

Recently in my attempt to question God, He reminded me of a time when he spoke to me. It was years later before what He spoke was brought to fruition.

Long story short, Dustin was working for a company where he was away from home every other week and missing out on a lot of things in our life. We had prayed for something to change so he could be home with our family. While I was seeking God about this matter, He said to me, "I am moving you." Girl, that scared me to death. My entire family lived near me and there was no way I would go anywhere. Besides, surely He didn't mean a *physical* relocation. In March 2011, I jotted that whisper in my journal and tucked it away. Fast forward to January 2014, God had removed Dustin from that job, and he was working a job where he was away even more. We were both growing weary and desperately needed a change.

One January evening, God spoke to Dustin, and he realized it was time to quit the job. Instead, he took a low-paying job at home while we sought the Lord for a miracle. A few months later in April of that year, Dustin received a phone call with the job offer of his dreams. The only downside: it required us to move. What? God was asking us to move?! I was sure He meant something else. But what's so incredible is in those three years of waiting, God had prepared our hearts and we knew this was what the Lord wanted for our family. This was the move He spoke to me about all those years earlier.

While it took what seemed like forever and I didn't understand how it could ever happen, God was making a way and put it into motion at just the right time. The Lord knew in March 2011 we were not ready, so He prepared our hearts until the time was right. I could talk for hours about what God has done in our life since our move, but I'll save it for another time. Just know this: it was just the right time. God's time is not our time, but He is faithful, and we can trust Him.

"For the vision is yet for the appointed time; It hastens toward the goal and it will not fail. Though it tarries, wait for it; For it will certainly come, it will not delay."

(HABAKKUK 2:3 CSB)

Daily Prayer:

Father, teach me island time. Every request I've made, every promise you've given, every answer you've sent on my behalf: I trust your timing. You see the bigger picture and I only see a sliver, so I trust your sight over mine. Lord, give me grace for the days I struggle to wait on you. Give me hope on the days that seem hopeless, and courage on the days that seem scary. Lord, I trust you. Your time, not mine. In Jesus name. Amen.

GODFIDENCE

My youngest son, Tyler, struggles a smidge with reading. It's a giant he's always faced. This school year we decided we were sick of staring the same giant in the face and tried a new approach to reading and IT WORKED! While he hasn't learned to read on his grade level yet, he is reading and doing it well. The thing I've noticed happening is that he is gaining confidence. Before, when asked to read, he would respond quickly with, "I can't read." Now, he's ASKING to read! He's even been willing to try reading at church in front of the other kids. Isn't it incredible what we can accomplish when we have a little confidence?

As I was thinking about my T-man, I couldn't help but think of a small shepherd boy named David. I feel like Tyler and David have a lot in common. Both small-built guys, a little scrappy, but not afraid of much. Each of them giant killers. While Tyler's giant came in the form of reading a book, I thought of David and the giants he faced as a boy, such as a lion, a bear, and a giant named Goliath. Don't you know it took some confidence to face each one?

David said to Saul,"Don't let anyone be discouraged by him; your servant will go and fight this Philistine!"

But Saul replied, "You can't go fight this Philistine. You're just a youth, and he's been a warrior since he was young."

David answered Saul: "Your servant has been tending his father's sheep. Whenever a lion or a bear came and carried off a lamb from the flock, I went after it, struck it down, and rescued the lamb from its mouth. If it reared up against me, I would grab it by its fur, strike it down, and kill it. Your servant has killed lions and bears; this uncircumcised Philistine will be like one of them, for he has defied the armies of the living God." Then David said, "The Lord who rescued me from the paw of the lion and the paw of the bear will rescue me from the hand of this Philistine."

Saul said to David, "Go, and may the Lord be with you."

(1 SAMUEL 17:32-37 CSB)

David understood it wasn't about what he could do, but about what God could do and the fact that He was with David. When David fought the lions and bears, God was with him, and God would be with him when he came face to face with the giant. David put his confidence in God because he *believed* God was able.

How often are we guilty of allowing the giants in our life to rule our possibilities? Yet if we would just put our confidence in a mighty God, the possibilities are endless. Apart from God, David never would have defeated a lion or a bear, and for sure not a mighty warrior who towered over him. But David knew the secret to success was believing in God for the impossible. David's confidence wasn't in himself, but in the God he served.

Are you apprehensive about stepping out in an area? If so, I have to ask: where does your confidence come from? It's time to believe God for the impossible. Maybe it's time to gain some Godfidence. God wants nothing more than to do crazy, awesome things through you, but do we believe He is able? It's time we believe again. It's time we get our Godfidence back.

"But Jesus looked at them and said to them, "With men this is impossible, but with God all things are possible."

(MATTHEW 19:26 CSB)

Daily Prayer:

Father, today I put my confidence in you. Today I agree that there is nothing I can do to face my giants: it's all you. Starting today, I choose to no longer try to figure things out on my own, but allow you full access to every part of my life. You, Lord, are how I fight my battles. In Jesus name. Amen.

DAY NINETEEN

THE OVERFLOW

I can still remember sitting in science class back in elementary school and learning about cause and effect for the first time. I was never very good or interested in science, but cause and effect were one of those things I found fascinating. With every cause, there is an effect. This blew my, elementary school mind. Then I heard about the Butterfly Effect. The Butterfly Effect is the concept that small causes can have significant effects. In Chaos Theory, The Butterfly Effect is the sensitive dependence on initial conditions in which a slight change in one state of a deterministic nonlinear system can cause substantial differences in a later state.

The theory is when a butterfly moves its wings somewhere in the world, it can cause a tornado or a hurricane in another part of the world.

How incredible is that? As I thought about this theory, God spoke to my heart, and it challenged me to ask some questions. Questions like, "what effect am I having? Do I truly understand the enormity of my decisions?" WOW! Those are some painful questions.

For the sake of this devotion, we will call the effects we have "the overflows". What is spilling out of you? What words, actions, or decisions are flowing from you? Every decision we make affects more than ourselves. We will do nothing that solely affects us. Our life choices flow from us and onto everyone around us, sometimes for generations to come.

Take Adam and Eve, for example. We are all seeing the effects of one wrong decision they made thousands of years ago. They made a poor choice, and it has affected everyone born from that day forward (Romans 5:12). Maybe you too can see the effects of someone else's mistakes overflowing into your own life. They were *oblivious* to how their poor judgment would affect those around them.

We've pointed out the hurt that can come from our poor choices, but disclaimer: the overflow isn't always negative. Take the most excellent example of all: Jesus. While sin entered the world through one man (Adam), Jesus took all the sin of the world upon himself and died on the cross for all of us. While sin came through one wrong decision, one act of love on the cross made life available to us.

What we do matters. Like a butterfly flapping its wings, our decisions have the power to change the course of history. You and Christ in you, can change the overflow.

What choices do you need to make today that will spill love, mercy, grace, and blessings onto those around you? Maybe it's time to break off the affair, or walk away from a toxic friendship. Perhaps you need to put down the bottle or throw out the needles. When Satan whispers the lie that it's too late or that you've gone too far, remind him to back up; he is fixing to get caught in the overflow of grace. Our effect changes the moment our cause changes.

> "See to it that no one fails to obtain the grace of God; that no "root of bitterness" springs up and causes trouble, and by it many become defiled."
>
> (HEBREWS 12:15 CSB)

Daily Prayer:

Lord, help me make wise decisions. I want the overflow of my heart to be that of mercy, grace, love and kindness. Make me aware of my poor choices and the affect they have on those around me. Jesus, show me your ways. Show me how to respond like you. In Jesus name. Amen.

SPEAK LIFE

I have a love-hate relationship with social media. Particularly Facebook. I rarely scroll through the feed because of all the garbage, gossip, unfiltered opinions, and discouragement I have to sort through to find a good post. I believe social media is an incredible tool Christians can use to bring life and hope to others. The question is: are we careful to use it this way?

This past week I was on one of my rare scrolls. During my scroll, I came across a post that seemed innocent until I noticed the dozens of comments. It intrigued me, what could people say about this seemingly insignificant post. I was heartbroken to read comment after comment of negativity. People talking down on others, giving their opinions about situations they knew little about, making someone else's business the highlight of their night and posting words intending to hurt others.

I climbed into bed that night frustrated about what I had read; disappointed that people, Christian people, would act like this, hurting others with their words, convinced they were right and others were wrong. It would have been super easy for this sassy girl to have given her two cents about the situation. I could've joined right in and to tell them how wrong they were, and it tempted me, for sure. My sassy mouth is undoubtedly one of my biggest struggles. But the more angry and disappointed I grew about the post, the more God whispered, "speak LIFE"!

> *"Not many should become teachers, my brothers, because you know that we will receive a stricter judgment. For we all stumble in many ways. If anyone does not stumble in what he says, he is mature, able also to control the whole body. Now if we put bits into the mouths of horses so that they obey us, we direct their whole bodies. And consider ships: Though very large and driven by fierce winds, they are guided by a very small rudder wherever the will of the pilot directs. So too, though the tongue is a small part of the body, it boasts great things. Consider how a small fire sets ablaze a large forest. And the tongue is a fire. The tongue, a world of unrighteousness, is placed among our members. It stains the whole body, sets the course of life on fire, and is itself set on fire by hell. Every kind of animal, bird, reptile, and fish is tamed and has been tamed by humankind, but no one can tame the tongue. It is a restless evil, full of deadly poison. With the tongue we bless our Lord and Father, and with it we curse people who are made in God's likeness. Blessing and cursing come out of the same mouth. My brothers and sisters, these things should not be this way. Does a spring pour out sweet and bitter water from the same opening? Can a fig tree produce olives, my brothers and sisters, or a grapevine produce figs? Neither can a saltwater spring yield fresh water."*
>
> (JAMES 3:1-12 CSB)

> *"From the fruit of a person's mouth his stomach is satisfied; he is filled with the product of his lips. Death and life are in the power of the tongue, and those who love it will eat its fruit."*
>
> (PROVERBS 18:20-21 CSB)

> *"Either make the tree good and its fruit will be good, or make the tree bad and its fruit will be bad; for a tree is known by its fruit.*

Brood of vipers! How can you speak good things when you are evil? For the mouth speaks from the overflow of the heart. A good person produces good things from his storeroom of good, and an evil person produces evil things from his storeroom of evil. I tell you that on the day of judgment people will have to account for every careless word they speak. For by your words you will be acquitted, and by your words you will be condemned."

(Matthew 12:33-37 CSB)

It's easy to speak life when everything is good. When everyone is treating you right and when the world agrees with us. On the flip side, when things get complicated when others words are hurtful, or when someone is against you - it's natural to want to speak anything but life into a situation. But can I remind you we cannot speak both blessings and curses; we are held accountable for everything we say, and what we speak we are full of.

If you want an abundant life — *speak* life! If you want to live a life full of dread and gloom speak… death. Before you decide, heed this warning: Don't expect God to bless when you speak life into yourself and death into your neighbor. It's time for us, (yes, me too), to rise above a Facebook post, a nasty email, a hurtful text, or the need to tear others down, and speak life. Speak life EVEN IF you think they don't deserve it. They too are God's children. He cares about His kids, even the ones who make mistakes! SPEAK LIFE!

Daily Prayer:

Today Lord, I ask you put your hand over my mouth and your love in my heart. God help me speak life into my situations and into the lives of those around me. God thank you for the power of life that I possess. Help me use my words wisely and for the building up of myself and others. Remind me that what I speak reflects who I serve. Help my lips be full of life. In Jesus name. Amen.

TANTRUMS AND TESTIMONIES

I marched. Okay, I stomped, down the stairs. It was somewhere between a two-year-old tantrum and an "I love Jesus" stomp. Others needed to know about my frustration and exhaustion.

I've thought about the power of our words a lot lately and how we can speak life and death into ourselves, our neighbors, and our situations. But after my stomping of the stairs, it challenged me to focus on the other side of that thought: my deeds.

> "And whatever you do or say, do it as a representative of the Lord Jesus, giving thanks through him to God the Father."
>
> (COLOSSIANS 3:17 NLT)

Did you catch that BIG word in the text; representative? God confronted me with this scripture after my tantrum. I particularly love this version and it spoke loud and clear to this girl. Not only are we to represent Jesus well with our words but also with our actions. OUCH!

There are MANY times where I, by some miracle, manage to hold my tongue, but my face says everything my tongue isn't. Take a few weeks ago as an example. Someone said something that frustrated me and I felt like they were a little harsh and out of bounds. My words were kind, but my face said everything I was thinking. After a bit, they apologized, but I needed to as well. While I SAID nothing wrong, my demeanor was wrong.

What's the point, Cassie? Well, the point is, we represent Jesus with our words and also our actions. You may say all the right things, but if your lip language doesn't support your body language, you might as well say what you're thinking.

So back to my tantrum. Dustin and I had gone away to celebrate our anniversary, and we ran into issues at the Airbnb we had booked. Each of our neighbors were super loud and very disrespectful of us old people trying to sleep before our long drive home the next day. I was super frustrated and even messaged the owner asking if there was anything she could do. I didn't receive a response, which made me more frustrated. So trying to be Christ-like, I chose not to say a word. How Christian of me, right? Well, not exactly. Instead, I waited until 6:30 am and was less than quiet as I packed and prepared to leave that morning. This led to the stomping of the stairs on my way out, hoping it disturbed them. I know, I know. No need to judge me, I've already repented.

In my mind, I had every right to stomp down the stairs, but the truth is I wasn't representing my Jesus very well. If those people didn't know Jesus, I guarantee I didn't help them find him.

How are you representing Jesus? Are you doing it in words, but not in deeds? Or maybe your actions are in check, but not your mouth. The two must go hand in hand. When we learn to represent Him well, we will reach more people and change more lives. Let's not be the reason someone runs from Jesus, rather than to Him.

Daily Prayer:

Father, today I ask you to forgive me for my poor representation. Sometimes I struggle to match my body language and my words. Lord, help me to always be mindful of my reaction toward others and mindful of who I am representing. I never want to be someone's reason for running from you. Help me express the same love I talk about with mouth, to my reactions and my body language. Thank you for grace when I get it all wrong. Keep working on me, Lord. I love you. In Jesus name. Amen.

DAY TWENTY-TWO

Ask Big

"Meanwhile, the boat was already some distance from land, bat-tered by the waves, because the wind was against them. Jesus came toward them walking on the sea very early in the morning. When the disciples saw him walking on the sea, they were terrified. "It's a ghost!" they said, and they cried out in fear.

Immediately Jesus spoke to them, "Have courage! It is I. Don't be afraid."

"Lord, if it's you," Peter answered him, "command me to come to you on the water."

He said, "Come." And climbing out of the boat, Peter started walking on the water and came toward Jesus."

(MATTHEW 14:24-29 CSB)

I have heard this story a bazillion times over my 30-plus years. It's a story most of us can quote word for word. We've heard it preached thou-sands of times, and it's a beautiful reminder of what happens when we have enough faith to step out of the boat. As I was reading through these passages like so many times before, something new about this account caught my attention. Now, I realize the thought I'm about to share isn't new, but it's something I didn't notice until recently. When I saw it, I knew God wanted me to share it with you. This thought of "Ask Big".

Let's take another look at verse twenty-eight.

"Lord, if it's you," Peter answered him, "command me to come to you on the water."

This, friends, blew my mind. Peter, knowing Jesus well and knowing the miracles He was capable of, asked Jesus to do something big. Right before this took place in the scripture, Jesus fed 5000 people with loaves of bread and fish. Peter had just witnessed another incredible miracle, so when Jesus came walking on water, Peter asked BIG.

"Hey Jesus! If it's you, why don't you have me come walk with you?" He knew the crazy, impossible things Jesus was capable of doing. Stepping out of the boat took faith, yes, but I beg to say that Peter had high hopes when He asked Jesus this request. Peter's first step of faith happened when he asked Jesus to do the impossible.

This is where I feel like we get stuck. We pray for faith that will move mountains and confidence to step out of the boat, but we never ask for the miracle. We want God to show up in remarkable and mighty ways, to do the impossible in our lives. Most of us even say we believe He is able. But yet, we never ask Him for the mighty, miraculous, and impossible. We want to see a miracle, but we're too afraid to ask for one. Instead, we play the "what if?" game. What if I pray for healing and it never comes? What if I ask for a financial miracle and I lose my home? What if I step out of the boat and sink? So rather than asking big, we keep our request to ourselves because we could look like fools if it doesn't happen the way we hope it will. Better yet, we worry about how God may appear if He doesn't deliver on our request. So, we sit silently.

Several years ago, I made a big request to God concerning my husband's job situation. Afterward, I believed with everything in me that God would deliver on my request. Some time later, I was visiting with a friend on the phone and she mentioned my husband's job. I told her he wouldn't be there much longer. She said, "Oh, so he got another job?" I laughed and said, "No, but he will have one soon." She was confused, and so I shared with her about my prayer. I explained I was choosing to believe and not doubt that God would provide the job. She thought I'd lost my mind and from that point on she didn't have much to do with me. No joke. But it wasn't a week or two later when God provided everything we had asked for. He performed a miracle.

The point is, we can believe He's able all day long, but we must have enough faith to make our request known to Him. Peter made a plea, and Jesus said yes. I understand that this will not always be the case. The "no's" have happened plenty of times in my life. However, when we align our desires with His desires, the answer is always "yes" (Psalm 37:4). If God is saying no to you, it's not because He doesn't love you. It's because He's God and He sees your life from beginning to end, and just maybe, you're making the wrong request. Regardless of if the answer is "yes", "no", or "not yet," have faith enough to ASK BIG.

Daily Prayer:

Lord, help me have no fear when praying big. Build my faith little by little until fear is gone and there is nothing left but faith that moves mountains. God, I believe you are big enough and strong enough to do above all I can ask or imagine. I believe that you want to do big and mighty things for me, in me, and through me. Help me, Lord, to not lose sight of the glory that is gained in the process and who it belongs to. In Jesus name. Amen.

SURVIVING THE DESERT: 101

Several years back, the hubs and I made the crazy decision to travel from Missouri, halfway across the country to California with our three kids all under age seven. It was insane. Oh, and I forgot to mention that we drove it straight through. All 26 hours. Even though my kids traveled like champs, I still have no desire all these years later to EVER do that again.

Now, if you're familiar with the west, you know that we drove through bookoo's of the desert on our trip. As we traveled state to state, we planned accordingly for pit stops to refuel the truck and ourselves. When the fuel gauge got to the half tank mark on the pickup, we stopped at the next station for gas. It could be hours in between stations to refuel and being stranded in the desert with 3 kids didn't sound to fun.

This week, God reminded me of the importance to prepare for the desert, spiritually. I'm sure I'm not the only one who has walked through a spiritually dry season or a desert as I like to call it. And it just so happens, I have recently come out of one. While I'm enjoying the view from the mountaintop, I realize that it's inevitable that I will once again go through another valley or desert. So how can I prepare for such a season? What steps can I take to make sure I come out of the desert full of joy and faith?

I wish I had a big list of incredible thoughts to rescue you from the season you're going through or may face, but I have just one: stay in constant communion with the Lord. That's it. It sounds so simple, doesn't it? Well, I wish it were as simple as it sounds. Living in constant communion with Jesus is a lifestyle. It isn't a list of to-do's, but it's making a choice to live every moment of every day with Jesus. Being in His word, filling yourself full of truth. It's choosing to be around people who build you up and encourage you in the faith. It's talking to the Lord throughout the day, sharing your thoughts and requests with Him. But it's also making time to sit at His feet and listen as He guides and directs your path through every season. The only way to come out of the desert full of joy is to be full of the Giver of joy.

When preparing for a trip across the desert, there are two things that you need to survive - food and water. I think we can all agree that these two items are essential and not just on a trek through the desert, but to survive. Period. This is true spiritually as well. To withstand a spiritually dry season, we must eat from the bread of life (John 6:35) and drink from the living waters of Jesus. (John 4:14)

The past two years have been some of the most challenging years of my life. I've walked, sometimes it felt more like a crawl, but I've been through the most prolonged desert and I often wondered if it would ever end. So when I speak to you today, know that I come to you from experience. I can honestly tell you, the ONLY thing that got me through that season was Jesus. And there were many days I didn't feel like being in community with Him, but determined, I pushed through, fought the good fight of faith and held onto the promises He made me. I decided there was no giving up, and no giving in, even if it took forever. Satan would NOT beat me in this.

Friend, I pray you're reading this from the mountaintop, but wherever you're at, there will come a time you find yourself in a dry place, prepare in advance. Don't wait until you're already going through it to be in constant fellowship with Jesus. Start today. Get so full of the bread and water, which is Jesus, that the desert doesn't stand a chance against you.

"If only you would prepare your heart and lift up your hands to him in prayer! Get rid of your sins, and leave all iniquity behind you. Then your face will brighten with innocence. You will be strong and free of fear. You will forget your misery; it will be like water flowing away. Your life will be brighter than the noonday. Even darkness will be as bright as morning. Having hope will give you courage. You will be protected and will rest in safety. You will lie down unafraid, and many will look to you for help."

(JOB 11:13-19 NLT)

Daily Prayer:

Jesus, I may not understand why I face the dry seasons, but ask you to use them to mold me. Use them to draw me close to you. Prepare my heart and draw me in now, before I face hard seasons. Teach me to rely on you and your words over my life. Teach me to trust you above all else. Teach me peace so I can be full of joy in a place with no joy. In your name I pray, Amen.

BE YOU

My goodness, have I been feeling super alone in my struggle of comparison. It seems like I've always struggled to be comfortable in my skin. At times it's hard to be the "me" God created me to be, rather than being "her." Do you ever struggle with this? I know Satan wants us to feel alone in our battles, but I'm willing to bet I'm not alone in this one.

I hate my urgent need to jump on social media each day, only to spend far too much time following other women or looking at others who are where I'd like to be in ministry, business, or life. Before long, to some extent, I'm wishing I were living her life rather than mine. I guess in some weird way, I want my life, but with her result.

As I have wrestled through my issues of comparison, God revealed to me a little thought. God whispered to me, "Cassie, stop trying to cheat." My heart became defensive. "Wait. What? What in the world do you mean? Cheat?" He said back to me, "Stop trying to do it like they do, or have what they have. I created you unique. Be YOU!"

Comparison is like taking a test. Maybe you remember back in school how a teacher may hand out a different test to each student, without the students' knowledge. Some may have test A, some test B, etc. Well, for kids like myself, that was a bad test day, because I would take an occasional peek at my neighbor's answers to help me along. It did me more harm than good. The same goes for now and comparing ourselves to others. You aren't meant to copy off of HER. God created you for YOUR life, YOUR gifts, YOUR ministry, YOUR family, YOUR… fill in the blank. God designed you to keep your eyes on your own paper. Trying to be someone else will cause more harm than good. You be you, I'll be me, and let HER be her.

God has way too big of a plan for you and I to spend our lives striving to be HER. BE YOU!

"I praise you, for I am fearfully and wonderfully made. Wonderful are your works; my soul knows it very well."

(*PSALM 139:14 ESV*)

Daily Prayer:

God, thank you for making me different from my neighbor. Thank you for assigning specific people to my path and giving me a special mission. I am so grateful you looked down and thought the world needed me. I am honored you created me just the way you did, with no mistakes. Lord, fix my eyes on you and not my fellow sister. I want to be everything you have in mind for me. Help me cheer on my sister as she is also unique and is a daughter to you. May my heart be pure and may no root of jealousy spring up within me. Show me who I am and lead me to be all you've created me to be. In Jesus name. Amen.

DAY TWENTY-FIVE

To Die For

"Tell me about yourself." How do you respond to this question? I've noticed, like myself, people often lead with a title, job position or what they do for a living. For instance, I might say, "I am a homeschool Mom of three crazy people." My husband, often leads with, "I work for KAMO power." Maybe you're able to say something super impressive like, "I own a multimillion dollar company." But you'll notice we tend to make it about what we do or how we make a living more so than *whose* we are. I can't think of a time I answered the previous question with, "I am a follower of Jesus." I mention the things I think gives me the most worth. Perhaps this is true of you too. I don't say just say "homemaker," I throw in homeschooling too. But, why? While I do it unintentionally, I guess it makes me feel more valuable in a way. Maybe I appear to have more worth if I mention my hard work as a homeschool Momma.

It appears we may put a little too much emphasis on what we do rather than whose we are. Maybe for you, someone called you worthless for so long, you believe it to be true. Maybe past mistakes or even current ones have told you you have no value. As God spoke to me about this topic, he revealed some of my own insecurities; my issue of never feeling like I'm enough. For far too long, I have allowed Satan to determine my worth, only believing what he says. My worth and your worth doesn't come from a paycheck, a person, or a position. Jesus measured our worth on the cross, with arms stretched wide, as Jesus took all the sin and shame from us and put it upon himself. He knew us, yet he loved us enough to stay on the cross.

> *"For God loved the world in this way: He gave his one and only Son, so that everyone who believes in him will not perish but have eternal life."*
>
> *(JOHN 3:16 CSB)*

EVERYONE. That means you. That means us. Despite what we have done or said, God still loved us enough to send Jesus to the cross in our place. Long before we were around to make mistakes and reject His love for us. Therefore, He must see a worth that we can't see ourselves.

> *"But you are a chosen people, a royal priesthood, a holy nation, God's special possession, that you may declare the praises of him who called you out of darkness into his marvelous light."*
>
> *(1 PETER 2:9 CSB)*

Royalty. Who would've thought we are God's special possession? It's time we put our worth in who God says we are, not in our titles, positions, people, or possessions. Jesus made it clear on the cross that our worth is immeasurable and our value more than we can fathom. No longer do we need to measure up to someone else's standards or look to fame, fortune, or our social media likes to determine our worth. Jesus made it clear. WE are to die for!

Daily Prayer:

> *Lord, thank you you have chosen me and given me a worth that man can't measure. Help me live life like I am your child, worthy of your love and sacrifice. May I be an offering to you, Lord, so that*

others may see you through my life. Lord, no longer will I look to others or accomplishments for value, because we can only find real value in your Son. You say I am worth dying for. Help me live like it. In Jesus name. Amen.

DAY TWENTY-SIX

REPURPOSED

Don't you just love Chip and Joanna Gaines? Or is it just me? They are my renovation heroes. So when we built our home a few years ago, I went Magnolia Farmhouse with it. I love Joanna's taste in decor and her willingness to repurpose old things and make them beautiful. While Fixer Upper is one of my favorite shows, I'm a fan of any renovation show. I love watching old things being made new.

Another renovation story I love is Saul's story of conversion to Paul in scripture. Saul, before he was Paul, was running around persecuting and killing Christians. Acts 8:3 tells us *"Saul, however, was ravaging the church."* He would enter house after house, dragging off men and women, and put them in prison. He was the worst kind of guy until one day, on his way from Jerusalem to Damascus, he encountered a man named Jesus.

"As he traveled and was nearing Damascus, a light from heaven suddenly flashed around him. Falling to the ground, he heard a voice saying to him, "Saul, Saul, why are you persecuting me?" "Who are you, Lord?" Saul said. "I am Jesus, the one you are persecuting," he replied. "But get up and go into the city, and you will be told what you must do." The men who were traveling with him stood speechless, hearing the sound but seeing no one. Saul got up

from the ground, and though his eyes were open, he could see nothing. So they took him by the hand and led him into Damascus."

(ACTS 9: 3-8 CSB)

In an instant, God took the worst of the worst and changed him from Saul, the murderer, to Paul, a new man. Paul turned thousands of hearts to the Christ he had persecuted for so long. God repurposed Paul, and He longs to repurpose you too. But, so often we get stuck thinking because we have a less than perfect past, we can never have a future. We believe the lie that after all we've done, God doesn't want us and he sure won't use us. I'm here to remind you, if He can take Saul, a murderer of God's people, and turn him into the Apostle Paul, a leader of God's people, he can and WILL use you too!

I don't know what kind of life you're living or what kind of history you have, but God is in the business of renovation. He wants to take your pain and your past and turn them into purpose. He wants to make a masterpiece out of your mess, turn your trials into a testimony and take your history and turn it into His-Story. He is the ultimate Fixer Upper, and He is waiting to make you new.

> *"Therefore, if anyone is in Christ, he is a new creation, the old has passed away, and see, the new has come!"*
>
> *(2 CORINTHIANS 5:17 CSB)*

Daily Prayer:

God, renovate me. No longer will I allow my past to determine my future. I may have started out on the wrong path, but I refuse to stay there. Lord, mold me. Make me into everything you want for me. Change my heart and my ways. Make me a leader of your people. Use me in ways I never saw possible. God, I am so grateful you are in the business of renovation. Make me new. In Jesus name. Amen.

I'VE GOT RHYTHM. BYE-BYE BLUES.

"Hurried people aren't happy people." I heard this quoted on a podcast and it struck me deep. It spoke right into a situation I'm praying about.

For months, God has been dealing with me about rest and rhythm. I finally understand how to take a real rest with Him, but that doesn't change the busyness of life. Rest doesn't cease all the commitments still staring at me. Instead, it allows me a place to go when the anxiety of the calendar weighs on me. So, I am grateful for rest in Jesus! But as thankful as I am for rest, I needed something more than rest. I began asking the Lord about His rhythm of life. I searched scripture for a hint of how He lived. From what I can tell, Jesus was also a busy man: always moving around, healing people and teaching others. He rarely had a moment by himself!

When I dug into scripture, I noticed that Jesus was a simple man. He didn't require many possessions, he had no permanent home, and He never took anything with him on his journeys, besides his disciples. Although He was busy and could have been more concerned with Himself and His needs, He was always joyful and available. This simple discovery led me to the following question: "How can I live this simple, joyful, available life in my busy world?"

I often beat myself up for the lack of time I have to connect with people during these busy seasons, whether it's friends, new families, or some days even the people in my home. With crazy schedules, it seems impossible and overwhelming to add one more thing to our calendar. But in my praying and searching for answers, God reminded me of a story in scripture:

> "They came to Jericho. And as he was leaving Jericho with his disciples and a large crowd, Bartimaeus (the son of Timaeus), a blind beggar, was sitting by the road. When he heard that it was Jesus of Nazareth, he began to cry out, "Jesus, Son of David, have mercy on me!" Many warned him to keep quiet, but he was crying out all the more, "Have mercy on me, Son of David!" Jesus stopped and said, "Call him." So they called the blind man and said to him, "Have courage! Get up; he's calling for you." He threw off his coat, jumped up, and came to Jesus. Then Jesus answered him, "What do you want me to do for you?" "Rabboni," the blind man said to him, "I want to see." Jesus said to him, "Go, your faith has saved you." Immediately he could see and began to follow Jesus on the road."
>
> (MARK 10:46-52 CSB)

Jesus, unlike myself, didn't look at his calendar or call meetings with His disciples to determine if there was time for this blind man. He simply ministered to him as He went along. This truth challenged me.

In this season of busyness I'm experiencing, I can still minister to others. It's as easy as ministering as I go. When I'm at a ball game, I can sit beside people I don't know and connect with a new family. While I wait for a practice to end, I can steal my hubby for dinner. When it's been a long week for a friend, and I'm preparing dinner, I can invite them over. I'm already cooking anyway, right? I am capable of being both joyful and available for those around me. Busyness doesn't have to mean unhappiness. I may not always be happy about the busy, but my calendar does not determine my joy. My happiness comes from the rest and the rhythm I find in the Lord. When I rest in the Lord, I learn His rhythm. I become effective in the kingdom, despite how busy I may be.

"Walk with me and work with me - watch how I do it. Learn the unforced rhythms of grace. I won't lay anything heavy or ill-fitting on you."

(MATTHEW 11:29 MSG)

Here's what this verse has taught me: the rhythm of Jesus is that of relationship, not works or rules. We put way more pressure on ourselves than Jesus ever would! News flash, there is not a right or wrong way to connect with others; just connect. Our relationship with others in this busy season doesn't have to be specific or perfect, it just needs to be full of grace. That's the rhythm of Jesus!

Daily Prayer:

Lord, help me notice others above myself in seasons of busyness. Put people on my path and make me keenly aware of them and their needs. Help me not focus on doing things perfectly and flashy, but with a heart of grace and need. I don't have to prepare a huge dinner and invite a new family over. I can connect with them any-where. Help me not focus on how but focus on the when. When will I connect? Remind me the answer is "now." Lord, I pray for an increase in energy and time management in this season. Lift me up, as I grow weary. In Jesus name. Amen.

DAY TWENTY-EIGHT

But What If

"**W**hat if?" This seems to be my go to line lately when visiting with the Most High. I feel like my prayer time often turns into convincing God that He's got the wrong girl. Surely He made a mistake when He went down His list of to-dos. Clearly, my name got mixed up with Cathy. It happens often enough, and I will bet God made a mistake! HA!

In all seriousness though, the "what if's" are an undeniable battle for me. The unknown is frightening and I'm doing my best to fight fear and just do it afraid. What a challenge that seems to be!

Recently, God revealed an idea to me. To be honest, I feel incapable of handling it. If I've ever needed faith, now is the time. I've asked the Lord more times than I can count, what if? "What if I fail? Lord, are you sure this is for me and for now? I have so many other obligations in my life, what if I can't manage it all?"

As I sought wisdom in His word, God reminded me of a time in scripture that Queen Esther likely had some, "what if" fears, that I too am facing. Let me tell you a bit about Queen Esther. Before Esther was queen, there was Queen Vashti. Her disobedience toward King Ahasuerus (Xerxes) cost her the crown. Vashti is removed, and this is where Esther's story begins. Esther was a beautiful, Jewish orphan who was raised by her cousin Mordecai. God strategically positioned her, an orphan, to be queen, and she is able to save her people.

I'd love to tell you all the details of her life, but for lack of space, you must read them for yourself. In short, Haman, the King's right-hand man, plots to kill all the Jewish people. That doesn't sit too well with Mordecai or Esther; they're Jews. So Esther has a choice to make: She can sit back and hope someone steps up to save her and the people, or she can take action herself as she is in the perfect position to do so. The Queen is well aware of what can happen if she disobeys the king's laws. Disobedience could mean death for her. However, despite the fear she likely faces, she knows what she must do.

> *"Go and assemble all the Jews who can be found in Susa and fast for me. Don't eat or drink for three days, night or day. I and my female servants will also fast in the same way. After that, I will go to the King even if it is against the law. If I perish, I perish."*
>
> *(ESTHER 4:16 CSB)*

I don't know what visions or dreams are staring you in the face, sweet friend, but I know God has plenty of them to go around. He isn't looking for perfect people who have life figured out; He's looking for obedient and willing people. I can imagine it terrified Esther. "What if I die?" She didn't let the unknown, the what if's, stop her. She pressed on, and God used her to save her people.

> *"Once again, on the second day while drinking wine, the King asked Esther, "Queen Esther, whatever you ask will be given to you. Whatever you seek, even to half the kingdom, will be done." Queen Esther answered, "If I have found favor in your eyes, Your Majesty, and if the King is pleased, spare my life; this is my request. And spare my people; this is my desire. For my people and I have been sold to destruction, death, and extermination. If we had merely been sold*

as male and female slaves, I would have kept silent. Indeed, the trouble wouldn't be worth burdening the King."

(ESTHER 7:2-4 CSB)

God wants to use you for something incredible. Will you allow Him to work through you or will you let the what ifs steal your vision? I plan to press on, even if I fail and even if I look foolish in the sight of man. Having faith is risky, but if there weren't a risk, you wouldn't need faith.

"If people can't see what God is doing, they stumble all over themselves; But when they attend to what he reveals, they are most blessed."

(PROVERBS 29:18 MSG)

Daily Prayer:

Lord, thank you for vision. Thank you for vision you've given me and vision to come. I know you have an excellent plan for my life and I want to follow your path. God, provide me with courage when you ask me to step out into faith. May I not ask, "what if I do," but "what if I don't?" There is a significant cost associated with hoarding the gifts, the favor and the plan you've given me. People's lives depend on what I do. Help me be brave in whatever you're asking of me. In Jesus name. Amen.

DAY TWENTY-NINE

WOE IS ME

"**A**ren't you gonna ask what happened?" said Ty.

"Well, actually, no, Ty. I was not," I proclaimed.

This was the conversation my youngest, and I had a few days ago. He and his brother had been wrestling, which turned to arguing and a fight between brothers. In the process, Ty got a bummed up eye. I saw the whole thing happen, so I wasn't too worried. When he headed to the freezer for the ice pack, I knew he would milk this for all its worth. It was fixing to turn into "poor me", and Tyler would do his darnedest to get Wyatt in trouble. So, like good mothers do, I ignored him; well, until he asked the question.

"Now when David and his men came to Ziklag on the third day, the Amalekites had made a raid against the Negeb and against Ziklag. They had overcome Ziklag and burned it with fire and taken captive the women and all who were in it, both small and great. They killed no one, but carried them off and went their way. And when David and his men came to the city, they found it burned with fire, and their wives and sons and daughters taken captive. Then David and the people who were with him raised their voices and wept until they had no more strength to weep. David's two wives also

101

*had been taken captive, Ahinoam of Jezreel and Abigail the widow
of Nabal of Carmel. And David was greatly distressed, for the people spoke of stoning him, because all the people were bitter in soul,
each for his sons and daughters. But David strengthened himself in
the LORD his God."*

(1 SAMUEL 30:1-6 CSB)

Like Tyler, David had every reason to cry, "woe is me." David had
lost everything he loved. He was devastated and had a right to be. He had
a right to mourn his loss, and he did so, for a time. Then we see the big,
"but". "But David strengthened himself in the Lord."

Maybe it occurred to him, "I can sit here the rest of my life crying
over my circumstances, or I can ask God to help me and trust He will take
care of what I'm going through".

Have you been there? I surely have. Recently I went through a situation that, to be honest, I wanted to give up on and play my pity card.
However, when I strengthen myself in the Lord, He reminded me I am
important and I matter to him. I no longer needed to question what others thought or didn't think of me. When I strengthened myself in the
Lord, nothing else mattered but the Lord's thoughts.

Maybe you relate. You are in a situation, and you deserve to have a
moment of sorrow, but friend, please don't get your mail there. God can
make beauty out of your brokenness. Not only does he want to, it's His
desire for you. Let's not allow the enemy to trap us in our sorrow, but let's
see what God says about our situation. That's just what David did. He
got up from his grief, wiped the tears from his eyes and inquired of the
Lord. The Lord then told him, "Pursue, for you shall surely overtake and
shall surely rescue." So David set out with 600 men to take back what the
enemy stole from him.

*"And when he had taken him down, behold, they were spread
abroad over all the land, eating and drinking and dancing, because
of all the great spoil they had taken from the land of the Philistines*

and from the land of Judah. And David struck them down from twilight until the evening of the next day, and not a man of them escaped, except four hundred young men, who mounted camels and fled. David recovered all that the Amalekites had taken, and David rescued his two wives. Nothing was missing, whether small or great, sons or daughters, spoil or anything that had been taken. David brought back all."

(1 SAMUEL 30:16-19 CSB)

Now, maybe you didn't catch this, but scripture says David not only got back what the enemy stole from him but also the plunder that the Amalekites had taken from others! He got it all, plus some! God gave him more than he asked. God wants to give you back more than you lost! Whatever it is the enemy has stole from you, God will replace, and He will probably give you more than you dreamed possible. (Joel 2:25-32) So whatever you are going through, don't drown in the sorrow, don't sit with the "woe me" attitude. Strengthen yourself in the Lord! You can trust Him to take care of any situation.

"The righteous cry out, and the Lord hears, and rescues them from all their troubles. The Lord is near to the brokenhearted; he saves those crushed in spirit."

(PSALMS 34:17-18 CSB)

Daily Prayer:

Lord, I've been in the world long enough to know that trouble is inevitable. When difficulty comes, give me the strength to endure, strength to fight the good fight, the strength that only comes from you. I don't want to get my mail at the house of sorrow. I want joy in my life, and I want abundance in my life. Remind me when hard days come, and the enemy is taking from me, that if I strengthen myself in you, if I persevere, you will give back all Satan has taken, plus a lot more. In Jesus name. Amen.

THE PROCESS

Process: a series of actions or steps taken to achieve a particular end.

As I settled in to write today, God spoke to me about Joshua. After the death of Moses, Joshua faced an enormous process as he set out to conquer the land promised to the Israelites. God did unimaginable, miraculous things because of the obedience Joshua had shown.

Joshua 3 - the miraculous crossing of the Jordan River.
Joshua 6 - the battle at Jericho.
Joshua 10 - the sun stood still.

These miracles were a byproduct of the opposition that stood between Joshua and the promised land. But I wonder, despite the miracles, as he went to battle day after day, did he question if the process he was enduring was worth the promise or if the said process would ever lead him to the promised land?

In my life, I often wonder the same thing. What I've noticed about most of us, myself included, is we want what God has for us but we want it now we don't want to wait. We want it easy, like a microwave dinner. When things aren't working out quickly or the way we believe they should, we assume we've heard Him wrong or we're being punished for something. But can I tell you, God doesn't allow trials in our lives to punish us. Rather, they are to propel us toward the promise.

When I first discerned the call to young adult ministry, God opened the door to teach a small group of around six people at the church I was attending. I was certain God would grow the group, but to my surprise, God moved us to a new church. For months I sat the bench, so to speak. I questioned time after time if I had heard Him correctly and if moving is what He wanted for me. In the process, I stayed faithful to His voice and moved churches. I taught once in the five months, before God moved us again, this time to a new town. Long story short, we moved. We got involved and sat the bench for another six months before God opened the door for my husband and I to step into the young adult ministry at our new church. I now realize God was growing, maturing, and teaching us how to handle the ministry He had for us. Sitting the bench for a year wasn't my idea of moving toward what God had for me, but he needed to prepare me to handle it.

> "Consider it a sheer gift, friends, when tests and challenges come at you from all sides. You know that under pressure, your faith-life is forced into the open and shows its true colors. So, don't try to get out of anything prematurely. Let it do its work, so you become mature and well-developed, not deficient in any way."
>
> (JAMES 1:2-4 MSG)

What would life had looked like for the Israelites if Joshua had given up in the process? What would my life and yours look like if we decided the process wasn't worth it? There's a process to your promise, but don't allow the process to rob you of your progress. God is working in your battles and in the pauses. Trust Him. Trust HIS timing. And trust HIS promise for your life.

Daily Prayer:

Today I trust you, Lord. Today I am choosing to believe that you have this all figured out. You haven't abandoned me or forgotten me. Your ways and your plans are perfect and strategic. While I can't wait to see the promise before me, I am happy to learn and grow right here, right now. The last thing I ever want, is to obtain the promise and lose it. Prepare me, Lord. Whatever you need to do, whatever steps you need to take to ensure I can handle what you have for me. In Jesus name. Amen.

DAY THIRTY-ONE

CAN YOU HEAR IT

"Lord, PLEASE. Give. Me. A. Sign"

Have you ever allowed these words to be your prayer? Girl, if I've prayed it once, I've prayed it a thousand times. You too? It all starts with you hearing or thinking you've heard God's voice, but you just need some confirmation— you need a sign. I believe God can and will perform mighty signs to get our attention, but His voice is more often a whisper, and it's meant to be learned. It's not a giant sign with His signature at the bottom telling us what to do, although I'd be cool with that.

Recently, I heard a little whisper from God, but I've needed some confirmation. I've spent months in prayer hoping for a sign full of directions and details. I just need to know for sure that's what He wants for me, you know? A little confirmation to make me more confident in His voice. But God, tired of me asking for signs, reminded me of a time when I begged for confirmation and His response.

My pastor had brought in a guest speaker to encourage our staff. This particular speaker has a great gift of prophecy, so with much anticipation, I waited for some confirmation through this man of God. He came and went, and while he was full of prophetic words for everyone there, he never had a word for me. Now I will be honest and tell you; I was not very pleased that God didn't provide the confirmation that I was so sure

I needed. So there I was, pouting and fussing to God about how I needed to hear from Him, but that didn't go as I planned either. God spoke to me at that moment and He reminded me of a time when He spoke, I listened, and His whisper came to fruition in my life. There was no significant sign, or confirmation needed. Then He said to me, "learn and listen to MY voice. I've already told you what you need to know, and you need to trust My voice. You don't need anyone else to tell you what I've already said." OUCH! That my friend was a hard truth to swallow. I needed to have faith in His voice.

In 1 Kings 19:1-13, we come across Elijah. Elijah is fearful and running for his life, he plopped down under a broom tree and prayed to die, he'd had enough. Sounds a lot like my pouting. Maybe not the dying part, but whining for sure. To be honest, there are times you will feel like giving up. Knowing Elijah needed a pick me up, God sent an Angel to feed him and give him the strength to go on.

> *"Then he said, "Go out and stand on the mountain in the Lord's presence." At that moment, the Lord passed by. A great and mighty wind was tearing at the mountains and was shattering cliffs before the Lord, but the Lord was not in the wind. After the wind, there was an earthquake, but the Lord was not in the earthquake. After the earthquake, there was a fire, but the Lord was not in the fire. And after the fire, there was a voice, a soft whisper. When Elijah heard it, he wrapped his face in his mantle and went out and stood at the entrance of the cave."*
>
> *(1 KING 19: 11-13 CSB)*

Our entire belief in God is built on faith, yet often we look for signs rather than listening for whispers. The very definition of faith is the substance of things hoped for, the evidence of things not seen (Hebrews 11:1). The voice of God requires our faith. We can see signs, but we can't look at His whispers. The still small voice requires faith to see and ears to hear. So how do we tune our ears to listen to the whisper? We spend time in

His presence. In the book of 1 Samuel 3, we find the story of Samuel when he was just a boy. The Bible tells us Samuel was lying in the temple of the Lord, where the ark of God was. He was lying in the presence of the Lord. The Lord spoke to Samuel three times, but each time Samuel thought it was Eli who was calling. When Eli realized what was happening, he told the boy it was the voice of the Lord he was hearing and he instructed him to respond, "speak for your servant is listening." Samuel was learning the voice of the Lord.

Can you hear it? The whisper. If you've felt like God isn't speaking, could it be that maybe you aren't listening? Or perhaps you need to spend some time laying in His presence? God wants nothing more than to whisper in your ear. He has an incredible plan for you, tune in and hear what He has to say.

Daily Prayer:

Lord, I understand your voice is something I learn. As a child learns their mother's voice, we too learn your voice. Teach me your voice. Lord, may I no longer ask for signs, but tune my ears to hear you. If I want to see my next step, I must learn to listen. Faith is by hearing, not by seeing. In Jesus name. Amen.

LIVING WITH EXPECTATION

Can I be transparent for a moment? I love Jesus with my whole heart. I crave time with Him. I believe He is a God of the impossible, and I can tell you story after story of the proof of it in my life. I have experienced His greatness and His love day after day. So, here I am, in love with Jesus, doing my best to love like Him and be like Him. Yet, most days I still struggle to believe His words over my life. I wrestle to think He can do something impossible even though He did the impossible less than 24 hours ago. I battle to live with expectation.

Recently I reached out to two, what I consider, big-time publications about freelance writing opportunities. I have been very excited about reaching out, but the problem I found is my lack of expectation. As I visited with a friend from church, I was excitedly telling him about reaching out to be a freelance writer for these publications but followed up by saying, "I don't expect to hear from them, but hey, I sent the emails." He could see the lack of faith I was carrying and kindly encouraged me to live in expectation. That's when I realized I never believed, not for a moment. Then came repentance. What does my disbelief say about the mighty God I serve? In one small sentence, I put a cap on God's greatness and on His ability to do extraordinary things for an ordinary girl.

As God has stirred my heart about this, I thought about Moses and the Israelites. Moses was brave enough to return to Egypt, but what if His faith stopped there? What if he doubted God could use him to rescue his people? What if he failed to expect God would do just as He promised? Would God still have used Moses to deliver the people? (Exodus 7)

This thought challenges me. How often have I gave up wondrous things because I don't believe God can do what I cannot? When Peter stepped out of the boat, and onto the water, I doubt he expected to sink. He took God at His absolute word and walked on water (Matthew 14:22-29).

I think too often, the problem hinges on our ability. I don't believe I will get the opportunity because I am too dependent on my own strengths, instead of on what God can do and what He wants to do in and through me. The freelance opportunities have very little to do with me or my ability and everything to do with God and His glory. Sure, it will bless me for God to use them, but ultimately it's about God's glory.

I don't know what area of your life needs some expectancy today, but I know the God of miracles and He wants to do incredible things in and through you. God needs you and me to believe He will do as He says He will. He wants to bless us, but we must believe He is able. Because HE IS ABLE!

Now to him who is able to do above and beyond all that we ask or think according to the power that work in us—

(EPHESIANS 3:20 CSB)

"But let him ask in faith without doubting. For the doubter is like the surging sea, driven and tossed by the wind,"

(JAMES 1:6 CSB)

Daily Prayer:

Father, I am waiting in expectation. I am full of faith today and believe what you have said about me and the things you've prepared before me. I will not doubt but look forward to the promises ahead. God, I understand the answer is not always "yes" but if I have heard you speak, I can wait with an expectancy like no other. Thank you, Lord, for your ways and your wisdom. In Jesus name. Amen.

CIRCUMSTANTIAL GOODNESS

The goodness of God. We sing about it, read about it, talk about it, but do we believe it for ourselves? I believe God is good. I believe He has a good plan for my life and that He does good in the lives of others until He isn't. Too often, I let the trials of life and my circumstances measure God's goodness. If life is good, then God is great. If life isn't so good, maybe He's not as good as I thought. When life is handing us lemons, we buy the lie that, if life isn't lemonade, God is the one passing out lemons.

"I've told you all this so that trusting me, you will be unshakable and assured, deeply at peace. In this godless world you will continue to experience difficulties. But take heart! I've conquered the world."

(*JOHN 16:33 MSG*)

Jesus reminds us that just because we are His followers, it doesn't mean we are exempt from life's difficult times. Now to be clear, God doesn't cause bad things to happen. The enemy is the one who's out to get us, not God.

"The thief's purpose is to steal, kill and destroy. My purpose is to give them a rich and satisfying life."

(JOHN 10:10 NLT)

God is good, even when circumstances are not. Please know, I'm not trying to make light of your current trials. I know what it's like to go through the trials of life. Maybe you're facing a diagnosis, marital struggles, losing a loved one or a drug addicted-teenager. I feel your hurt, and the trials you encounter are real and painful, but even amid the darkest trials our circumstances do not determine God's character. God is good even when things are not.

"Give thanks to the LORD, for he is good; his faithful love endures forever."

(PSALM 107:1 CSB)

"The LORD is good to all; he has compassion on all he has made."

(PSALM 145:9 CSB)

"And Jesus said to him, "Why do you call Me good? No one is good except God alone."

(MARK 10:18 CSB)

"You are good and do good; Teach me Your statutes."

(PSALM 119:68 CSB)

The Bible is full of verses about God's goodness, written by people who experienced trials and tribulations just like you and me. I thought about the words of Jesus: *"no one is good but God."* He said this knowing His Father had sent Him here to die. I wondered if I could believe my father was good if he brought me into the world to die for people I'd never even met. I'm sure Jesus didn't necessarily think His imminent death seemed like a good day *(Luke 22:41-44)*, but He trusted that even though it looked bad, it wouldn't end bad. He knew God was good and He would bet His life on it. I know things may not look good for you but God is good and *all things work together for the good of those who love God and are called according to his purpose (Roman 8:28)*. Don't give up. Don't stop believing in God's goodness. He is with you, and He is for you.

Daily Prayer:

Father, help me. It's so easy to look around or watch the news and become fixed on all the terrible things going on in my life and in the world. Lord, I want to fix my gaze on you and on your goodness. I want to walk through my trials with my chin up and joy in my heart. Saying YOU'RE good and believing it are totally different. I want to believe in your goodness. I want to shout YOUR praises, even on my darkest days. God, thank you-YOU are walking with me through this life. Thank you for the life you have so freely given to me. Help me walk through it. Bring joy and goodness back to my life. In Jesus name. Amen.

RUSH THE WAIT

S everal years ago, Dustin, and I were struggling in our finances. He had quit a job a few months earlier and had been working for much less pay than his previous job. Now, let me say, I know with everything in me that him quitting his job was God ordained. He isn't one to just up and leave a job. However, knowing the Lord had ordered our steps, didn't change the struggle we were in. We drowned in worry, and felt like God couldn't hear our cries for help. It seemed as if He was too far out of reach to listen to us. When the financial storm raged against us, we decided that maybe we had heard wrong and perhaps the job change wasn't right. Within days, Dustin was on the phone with my brother, making plans to work for him in Texas. He would spend the next 40 days away from our family, and we continued that vicious cycle for about a year.

It didn't take us long to realize that the initial job change was, in fact, God ordained, but we became a little too impatient when the storm raged on our finances. We became God over our situation. We decided He wasn't working as quickly as we'd like, so we took control from Him and did things our way. In Exodus 24, God called for Moses to go up to Mt. Sinai alone to receive his commands and leave Aaron in charge of the people. We are told he was there for 40 days and nights.

Meanwhile, the people decided Moses was taking too long, and they went to Aaron saying, "*come make gods for us who will go before us because this Moses, the man who brought us up from the land of Egypt—we don't know what has happened to him.*" Long story short, they couldn't wait any longer for God, so Aaron took their gold jewelry and made an idol out of it. Just like Dustin and I couldn't wait on God any longer, we created our own god that would get things done and in our timing.

I'd love to tell you we saw what we had done, changed our minds, and that life was all good. But I can't. We recognized what we had done, but our actions caused a ripple effect, and we felt stuck. Sometimes we have to live with the consequences of our actions. Our particular outcomes meant Dustin was on the road for a year. He was rarely home with our family and missing all the little things in life. His absence also meant a strained relationship for the two of us, along with so many other issues, all from our poor decision to rush the wait.

I know the wait can be painful and scary. Believe me, when we got our hearts right and asked God to get a handle on the mess we made, it was still difficult and scary. God didn't swoop in and immediately pull us out of the chaos. Again, we waited, but this time we didn't rush the wait. We decided to put God in his rightful place, no matter what that looked like. We trusted Him and His timing for our life. After about a year on the road, Dustin felt God dealing with him to walk away from that job and be at home. Again, this meant he'd be making much less money. However, we were ready this time. Not financially, per se, but were spiritually ready to trust God. We knew God had a plan. We just had to be still and wait on Him. Within a few months, Dustin received a call for the job he'd always dreamed of. God's timing could not have been more perfect.

I understand that when you are in the wait, it seems like it may never happen… but God! God always has a perfect plan and He is never late. Don't allow your fears to rush the wait. Give God all control.

"Wait for the Lord; be strong, and let your heart be courageous. Wait for the Lord."

(PSALM 27:14 CSB)

Daily Prayer:

Lord, teach me to wait. Waiting is hard, faith is hard. When I'm ready to give up and create an idol for myself, remind me that your ways are better. Give me the strength, courage, and endurance to withstand the wait, however long it may be. Put Godly people in my path to encourage me in the delay. God, I am so thankful to know that when I'm in that season of waiting, it's because you are busy work all things out for me. In Jesus name. Amen.

LOST IN TRANSLATION

Recently on a flight, I had the privilege of sitting next to a sweet little foreign woman, we'll call her Molly (although Molly sounds extra American). I can only assume she was sweet because of endless smiles she passed my way and what her daughter told me about her. Molly didn't speak or understand any English except to say, "I don't speak English".

It was a rather frigid flight. I'm pretty sure the airlines enjoy playing freeze out with their passengers. As I sat curled inside a beach towel with my fuzzy socks in tow, I couldn't help but notice Molly shivering. After a few minutes passed the stewardess went around with blankets (not the free ones of course, but the ones that will cost you an Alexander Hamilton... that's a ten-dollar bill for those of you who are still trying to figure it out). Molly was quick to snatch a blanket off the cart while it rolled by, and the stewardess stopped to ask for payment. But, there was a problem: Molly didn't speak or understand any English. It didn't take the flight attendant long to get flustered and become hateful with her. Eventually, she snatched the blanket back from Molly and walked away. I was heartbroken for the woman and the treatment she endured because of the lapse in translation. Molly wanted that blanket pretty badly because she quickly hopped up and ran to the back of the plane where her family was seated to explain to them, in her language what was going on. Her son-in-law kindly took care of the situation, and soon, she was snug as a bug in a rug in her new blanket. After all the madness, I spent the duration of my flight doing my best to help her understand when it was time to eat or drink. I didn't want her to feel condemned or left out because she misunderstood.

As I sat there, God dealt with my heart about how often I have the same attitude as the stewardess. The "I don't understand you, so it's my job to condemn you," attitude. A Pharisee-like manner. The body of Christ has stood in judgment for so long, that we've given ourselves a bad rap. We spend way too much time judging people's actions because we don't understand how or why they could do what they do. All the while giving up the love Jesus has called us to share. It reminds me of the story about the adulteress woman.

> *"At dawn he went to the temple again, and all the people were coming to him. He sat down and began to teach them. Then the scribes and the Pharisees brought a woman caught in adultery, making her stand in the center. "Teacher," they said to him, "this woman was caught in the act of committing adultery. In the law Moses commanded us to stone such women. So what do you say?" They asked this to trap him, in order that they might have evidence to accuse him. Jesus stooped down and started writing on the ground with his finger. When they persisted in questioning him, he stood up and said to them, "The one without sin among you should be the first to throw a stone at her." Then he stooped down again and continued writing on the ground. When they heard this, they left one by one, starting with the older men. Only he was left, with the woman in the center. When Jesus stood up, he said to her, "Woman, where are they? Has no one condemned you?" "No one, Lord," she answered. "Neither do I condemn you," said Jesus. "Go, and from now on do not sin anymore."*
>
> *(JOHN 8:2-11 CSB)*

Jesus stood up for this woman, not because He agreed with her life-style or because He understood her choices. He was the only one left and the only one who could rightfully sling a stone at her, but He didn't. Jesus saw who this woman could be if loved and forgiven. He laid out the blueprint for you and I. There is not one of us who can rightfully judge another.

"We have all sinned and fallen short of the glory of God"

(ROMANS 3:23).

What we can do though, is love one another, encourage one another, and pray for one another. We will never understand, nor do we need to know how someone could intentionally hurt others or live the lifestyle they choose to live; but we can love them through it. We can show them a better way. We can show them the love of Christ.

"Above all, maintain constant love for one another, since love covers a multitude of sins."

(1 PETER 4:8 CSB)

Daily Prayer:

Father teach me, love. Lord, help me understand I am not in this world to judge it but to love it. With a poor attitude toward my neighbor, I will never lead them to YOU. I don't have to agree with my neighbor's lifestyle, but I can still love my neighbor. God, teach me to live out the command to love my neighbor as myself. By "neighbor", that means everyone I meet, pass, and come in contact with. Help me love like you love. In Jesus name. Amen.

LET IT RAIN

Recently my daughter, Annah, and I went on a mommy-daughter getaway to one of my favorite places; Maui. I was super excited to share with her one of the most incredible places on earth, and to spend the week connecting with my gorgeous, not so little, girl. Maui and I have a special relationship. Maui is where I first heard God whisper to me to write, so I hold Maui pretty close to my heart. Pumped to be there with my girl, I was also pumped and desperate to hear from God. I needed a change of pace, and I love being near the water. It doesn't matter if it's the river, lake, or ocean, I seem to connect with Jesus more closely when near water. Do you have a special place where you hear him a little louder? For my husband, it's in the woods while he hunts deer and turkey. Author, Mark Batterson, refers to these places as whispering spots.

For two years, I have been praying about a specific desire of mine. I needed to hear from God on this one. It's a "crazy" desire and I've prayed so hard for God to make it a reality, yet it hasn't seemed to happen. So, I changed the way I approached it in prayer. Rather than praying for God to make it happen, I asked Him to remove any dream I had that wasn't His desire. That was a tough prayer to pray. His desire or not, I wanted this dream. However, spiritually, I know His desires are always more incredible than my thoughts. If it isn't His desire, it's because He has something far more significant for me. So, I kept on praying this same simple prayer: "Lord, remove any hope, dream, desire, or vision that isn't yours."

I was anticipating getting to one of my whispering spots and hopefully learning what God's desire, or lack thereof, was for me. Day after day, I would pray my prayer, and day after day, God revealed to me things that caused my desire to wither. He highlighted things that I never considered and the things that illuminated the selfishness of my dream. It wasn't long before my desire became less important to me, and I surrendered my ways, my thoughts, my plans, and my desires to Him.

Fast forward two weeks later. I was enjoying a fantastic worship service at church hands held high as I sang, "Let it rain, open the floodgates of heaven, let it rain." As I sang this chorus over and over, God spoke to my heart. He whispered, "hold open your hands," so I opened my hands, palms up. He said to me, "because you have opened your hands, I can take what I want and give to you what I will." I had consumed myself for so long with a dream that wasn't for me, that I nearly missed what God intended for me. When we go to God with a clenched fist, He isn't able to give to us. He needs us to come with our hands wide open. While He may take some things from us, it's only so our hands can hold all He has to give.

I don't know what your dreams look like, but I know if you want the answer to always be "yes" you need to align your thoughts with His desires.

> Delight yourself in the LORD; And He will give you the desires of your heart.
>
> (PSALM 37:4 CSB)

When we let the Lord satisfy us, it's then we will want what He wants. It's then, He will give us His desires.

I want to ask you two questions. I hope that this may help you determine if your desire is His or yours. I am praying for you. I'm believing God for fulfillment in your life, and that it birth His desires within you.

Question's to consider:

1. What is the "why" behind your desire? If all your whys begin with I, it may be nothing more than selfish ambition.
2. Who pays the cost? I don't necessarily mean money, but if your desire costs your spouse and your children and only benefits you, it may not be God's heart for you.

"Trust in the Lord with all your heart, and do not rely on your own understanding; in all your ways know him, and he will make your paths straight."

(Proverbs 3:5-6 CSB)

Daily Prayer:

Lord, I stand here today, hands open wide. Take what YOU want and give me what YOU will. Align my desires with YOURS and remove anything that isn't for me. I want what YOU want for me. Mold me and make me. Prepare me for great things. In Jesus name. Amen.

MADE FOR MORE

H ave you ever wondered if there is more to your life? Do you have a purpose? If so, what is it? Or maybe you're "living the life," so to speak, and you aren't too concerned if there's more because from where you sit, life couldn't be better. No matter where you're at, scripture assures us that God has a plan and a purpose for each one of us.

> "For I know the plans I have for you," declares the Lord, "plans to pros-
> per you and not to harm you, plans to give you hope and a future."
>
> (JEREMIAH 29:11 CSB)

What captivates me about this scripture, isn't the promise of a plan for us, but that the Jewish people were in captivity when God gave them this promise (Jeremiah 29:10). They had been living a life apart from God, and when God gave Jeremiah this word, they were in exile to Babylon. This truth confirms two things to me:

1) God loves us, even when we live apart from Him and
2) He has a plan for us, despite who we've been, who we are, or where we are.

I feel like, so often, we believe the enemy's lie that we can be nothing more than we are right now. We buy into the lies. We think because our parents were one way, we will be too. Maybe you struggle with addiction, and you've chosen to believe you can be nothing else but an addict. We accept the lie as truth.

I want to remind you, things didn't look promising for the Jews either in Babylon, but God had a plan for them, even then, in the mess they had created for themselves; and He has a plan for you too.

Our job, the Great Commission, is to tell the world about Jesus. We all have the same purpose, but our approach looks different for each of us. Your gift may not be to write about it, but mine is. God planned for me to write to you, even when I was living a life of sin and wanted to be as far from Him as possible.

I know living God's plan for your life sounds a bit cliché, but it is possible, and rewarding, not just in this life but also in the one to come. So, how do you know God's plan for you?

> *"Then you will call on me and come and pray to me, and I will listen to you. You will seek me and find me when you seek me with all your heart."*
>
> *(JEREMIAH 29:12-13 CSB)*

Short answer: Seek Him with ALL that you are. He is ready and waiting for you. He wants nothing more than to give you a life you never dreamed of and He longs for you to reach people that seem unreachable. I never imagined I would be a writer. I bet my high school English teachers didn't either. But, when we let God plan our life, there will be *many* pleasant surprises.

Daily Prayer:

> *God, surprise me. Give me dreams and visions of the plan YOU have for my life. Forgive me of the sin I have hidden and make me new. Give me a new heart and a new desire for YOU. Give me the desire to walk in YOUR ways and live out the plan YOU have for me. In Jesus name. Amen.*

MY CONTENDER

You may find this hard to believe, but I've always been a bit of a spit-fire. While I've come a long way in this area, there's one thing that will set me off quicker than I like to admit: messing with my babies. You want to see momma bear? Mess with my cubs. And if you're a momma, you said… "Amen, sister!"

Maybe you've been in a situation that left you feeling the need to fight? Perhaps verbally or emotionally? Maybe someone has wronged you or criticized you on some level. Or perhaps it's worse than that, and they've hurt someone you love, like a child or a spouse. I'm sure at some point we've all been there.

Over the past couple of months, I have been under a slight spiritual attack, and it seems as if it's been with people.

My husband and I have stepped out in faith in a few different areas, and we recognize Satan longs to bring us down because of it. Knowing my lifelong struggle with rejection, he realizes people are the best way to steal my joy and send me packing far away from where God wants me to be. Throwing in the towel and allowing Satan to win this battle would be easy. But to his dismay, I am way more stubborn than he gives me credit for. So, how do we fight? How do we send Satan packing and still love the people who hurt us in the process? I believe we don't.

Wait. What? Aren't we supposed to fight the good fight of faith? Sure. But when Satan is coming against us, we will exhaust ourselves trying to resist, so, we give it over. We let Jesus fight our battles.

> *"Contend, O Lord, with those who contend with me;*
> *fight against those who fight against me!"*
>
> *(PSALM 35:1 CSB)*

> *"Awake, and rise to my defense!*
> *Contend for me, my God and Lord."*
>
> *(PSALM 35:23 CSB)*

This, my friend, is how *we* fight our battles. We let God fight for us. When we pray, He fights. The word "contend," in this setting of scripture, is the Hebrew word "Riyb" it means to battle physically and verbally.

Mark Batterson, author of *Draw the Circle*, explains it like this: "*It refers to both physical combat and verbal combat. So it runs the gamut from cage fighting to courtrooms. God is both a mother bear (don't mess with His children) and a defense attorney (pleading our case)."*

We do not need to defend ourselves against naysayers and Pharaoh's who live life determined to drag us down and impede on what God wants for us. We are God's children, and He has our back.

> *"If God is for us, who can be against us?"*
>
> *(ROMANS 8:31 CSB)*

But does allowing God to fight for us immediately remove the anger or bitterness we may feel? No, like everything else in life, it's a process. When anger arises, so should prayer. Little by little, the irritation, resentment, hurt, rejection, and the offense, will all fade away until all that's left is love. I encourage you today, hit your knees and allow God to fight for you. We win our greatest victories when our knees hit the floor.

Daily Prayer:

"Contend, O Lord, with those who contend with me; fight against those who fight against me!" Fight my battles because I can't do it on my own. Give me strength to endure the trials and remind me YOU are working in my situations. YOU, God, are my defender. YOU have conquered death, hell, and the grave. I know YOU can defeat my enemies. In Jesus name. Amen.

BLINDED BY THE SIGHT

I love the way a salad looks. I realize that's an odd way to kick off this devotion, but go with it for a moment. Salads look delicious and oh so pretty. I am always so tempted to try a big bite. They are colorful and crunchy looking. They appear to be pure deliciousness. But to me, they taste terrible! I am tempted more times than you can imagine by a beautiful salad only to spit and sputter after one bite. My salads are comprised of cheese and croutons, hold the lettuce and everything healthy.

I've been reading through the book of Judges lately and I ran into the story of Samson. Samson is well-known for his strength and his betrayal by Delilah. But another pattern I noticed was Delilah wasn't the only woman Samson fell for. He loved *all* the Philistine ladies.

"Samson went down to Timnah and saw a young Philistine woman there." "then he went and spoke to the woman because she seemed right to Samson."

(JUDGES 14:1,7 CSB)

"Samson went to Gaza, where he saw a prostitute and went to bed with her.

(JUDGES 16:1 CSB)

"Sometime later he fell in love with a woman named Delilah, who lived in the Sorek Valley."

(Judges 16:4 CSB)

After reading through the book of Judges, I've concluded that Samson had a sight problem. Not because the Philistines gouged his eyes out (Judges 16:21); he had a sight problem long before that. In Judges 14, God's Word says the young Philistine woman seemed right— she looked good to Samson. The prostitute looked good. Delilah looked good. Every woman Samson encountered *seemed* right. Yet it cost him his strength, his gift from God, and ultimately his life.

Samson had me wondering: how often do we face things that seem right, yet if we are not prayerful, can lead us astray? Can I speak to my wifey friend for a moment? The guy at the office who seems to understand you more than your husband does; the relationship may feel right but it isn't. God's heart is *for* your marriage, not against it. To my single friend, looking for Mr. Right. You may find someone who seems like they've got everything you've ever imagined, but if they will compromise your Christ-minded values, they aren't right for you.

Friend, the web is full of what seems right and appears good, but let me clarify: it *is not* good. It does nothing but rob you of real relationships with loved ones and the ones you have the potential to love. These seemingly good things have only one mission: to destroy you, your relationship with Jesus, and your relationship with others. My point is, not all that looks right and good is right and good.

Don't allow the picture the world paints to steal your sight away from the creator of the world. Not everything that seems right *is* right. Prayerfully consider the decisions you are making because making a decision based on an outer appearance may leave you spitting and sputtering, just like my salad. Seek godly counsel from good, godly mentors.

Where no counsel is, the people fall: but in the multitude of counselors, there is safety.

(*PROVERBS 11:14 CSB*).

Prayerfully consider your decisions and actions, sweet sister. Don't let the fleeting beauty of sin lead you astray.

"By faith Moses, when he was come to years, refused to be called the son of Pharaoh's daughter; Choosing rather to suffer affliction with the people of God, than to enjoy the pleasures of sin for a season; Esteeming the reproach of Christ greater riches than the treasures in Egypt: for he had respect unto the recompence of the reward."

(*HEBREWS 11:24-26 CSB*)

Daily Prayer:

Father, blind ME with YOUR love. Keep my gaze fixed on YOU. Put people in my path who will counsel me and encourage me to walk with YOU. Lord, remove relationships that aren't of you from my life. Allow my eyes to see through your lens into every situation and relationship. In Jesus name, Amen.

DAY FORTY

IN NEED OF RESCUING

Water swirled around my body like a whirlpool. My senses para-
lyzed as I stood pinned to a tree root. Darkness surrounded my
family as the boat, and the gigging lights, disappeared. Left with only the
glow of the lunar halo surrounding the moon. That January night seems
so long ago now, but I think back to the accident on Current River and
how God reached down and pulled my family out of the dark waters.

As I thought about that night, I wondered how many other times in
life God has pulled me out of the darkness. We are by nature sinful people, and therefore; we do sinful things.

> *"Now the works of the flesh are obvious: sexual immorality, moral*
> *impurity, promiscuity, idolatry, sorcery, hatred, strife, jealousy,*
> *outbursts of anger, selfish ambitions, dissensions, factions, envy,*
> *drunkenness, carousing, and anything similar. I am warning you*
> *about these things—as I warned you before—that those who prac-*
> *tice such things will not inherit the kingdom of God."*
>
> (GALATIANS 5:19-21 CSB)

WOW! That's a heavy list that Paul mentions here. I understand that
you don't fit into most of this list, but you fit in somewhere we all do.

There are so many areas that idolatry alone covers: money, success, sex, family need I go on? What about selfish ambition? Or maybe jealousy hits home for you. I'm not here to point out all your flaws. I just want to point out the fact that WE are all in desperate need of a Savior. We all need rescuing.

When God graciously sent his Son to die on a cross for us, it wasn't so we would continue to live in darkness and sin. He sent his Son so we could have life and life abundantly (John 10:10). There is something miraculous that happens when we surrender our lives to Christ. In all my years as a Christ follower, I've made plenty of mistakes and lived in my fair share of sin. However, the more I surrender, the less sin is a struggle in my life. I will never be free of sin in this life, but I will definitely strive for it.

While verses 19-21 talk about living by the flesh, if we continue reading, we learn what living by the Spirit looks like.

"But the fruit of the Spirit is love, joy, peace, patience, kindness, goodness, faithfulness, gentleness, and self-control. The law is not against such things. Now those who belong to Christ Jesus have crucified the flesh with its passions and desires."

(GALATIANS 5:22-24 CSB)

We needed rescuing, and God made a way through Jesus Christ. No longer do we have to live in darkness, but God calls us into His marvelous light. (1 Peter 2:9).

"For everyone who calls on the name of the Lord will be saved."

(ROMANS 10:13 CSB)

Call out to Him and let Him rescue you; let Him make you a new creation (2 Corinthians 5:17). We no longer have to live in sin or by the flesh, we have the Spirit of God living inside of us.

"He reached down from heaven and rescued me; he drew me out of deep waters."

(PSALMS 18:16 CSB)

Daily Prayer:

God, rescue me. Save me from the darkness that is my life without you. Bring me into the light and into right relationship with YOU. Forgive my fleshly living and put YOUR spirit inside of me today. Thank you for sending your Son for me. Starting now, I will live by the spirit. In Jesus name. Amen.

PARENTAL GUIDANCE

Several years back, I worked through *Not a Fan*, a bible study by Kyle Idleman. Much of that study has stuck with me over the years, but for this devotion, I want to highlight one particular thought. Kyle was talking about a man whose daughter had grown up and left the church and her faith. The father said something I'll never forget, "*I raised her in church, but I didn't raise her in Christ.*"

As a parent, this challenges me. My kiddos are growing up too fast, and I'm understanding the pain my parents went through of raising my crazy siblings and I. Parenting is hard work. Some days, I fail so hard. I get frustrated and sometimes raise my voice. I spend too much time focused on everything else, that I can't remember if we've even connected that day.

As if that's not bad enough, I'm also guilty of letting the little things become big things. Like a few days ago, when I became upset with my oldest for allowing our dog inside with dirty paws, leaving tracks across my white rug. It frustrated me; the lack of thoughtfulness toward the house cleaner (AKA momma).

Right after I finished having myself a little tantrum, I received a text message from one of my dear friends asking for prayer. Some of her family had been in a terrible accident with their church youth group in which three teenagers lost their lives. Talk about a change of perspective. At that moment, I looked at the young man I was ready to whoop just moments before and became so thankful he was still with me and able to make messes (and just a side note here: you don't have to be a parent for this to apply. Maybe you're a grandparent, auntie, school teacher, mentor, babysitter. You impact the children around you. And a duty to show them the love of Jesus.)

I am far from having this mom thing figured out, but as the Lord challenges me, there are some things I am learning. There are many things the Lord is teaching me, but the most important and life-changing goes back to the Bible study and what was said.

Raise up your children in Christ. Just showing up to Sunday morning service isn't the answer and beating them with the Bible will not work either. Making them memorize the Torah won't work, but living out our faith, day after day... that will change everything. Loving our kids like Christ loves us shows them a genuine faith, a faith they will always come back to. When I react with anger and put everything else ahead of my children, I'm not emulating Christ very well. Some days that love comes in the form of an "I'm sorry". Sometimes it happens by saying "no" to others, so I can say "yes" to my kids. Often, it's an extra long hug and an encouraging word. It's not losing your cool when they share their struggles, but loving them just like Jesus loved the prostitutes and tax collectors. This kind of love is never easy, but it is a must. And we absolutely believe in spankings, but we also believe in the love of Jesus.

I don't know what your parenting struggle is, but when you build your home on the foundation of Christ and His love, you CAN'T fail. Your children, my children, will make mistakes and let us down. They will drive us bonkers more often than not, but how will we respond? We only get one chance with them, and friends, life is so swift. Tomorrow isn't promised. May we make the most of the days we have and love them like Jesus.

*"Unless the Lord builds a house, its builders labor over it in vain;
unless the Lord watches over a city, the watchman stays alert in*

vain. In vain you get up early and stay up late, working hard to have enough food— yes, he gives sleep to the one he loves. Sons are indeed a heritage from the Lord, offspring, a reward. Like arrows in the hand of a warrior are the sons born in one's youth. Happy is the man who has filled his quiver with them. They will never be put to shame when they speak with their enemies at the city gate."

(PSALM 127:1-5 CSB)

Daily Prayer:

Lord, thank you for the opportunity to be a mother, an aunt, a grandmother, a mentor who can pour into and direct a child's life. Lord, help me keep my focus on YOU, so I don't lead my children in the wrong direction. God, help me put YOU and YOUR priorities before all else. Help me raise these children YOU'VE entrusted to me in Christ, not just in a church house. In Jesus name. Amen.

SAWDUST BROWNIES

"Cassie, have you tried these brownies? They are delicious."
That was a lie straight out of my dear friend's pie hole.

My friend Faith*, seems all sweet on the outside, but inside she is full of jokes and trickery, such as getting me to eat, what I now call, "sawdust brownies". I'm not lying when I say, it took me ten minutes to chew and swallow that brownie. It tasted and felt like someone had poured sawdust right into my mouth. Worst. Brownie. Ever.

If you're wondering - Yes, I know what sawdust tastes like. I grew up in a family of saw-millers and construction workers. Those brownies may have looked good, but I assure you they were not good.

Earlier this week, I started a new Bible plan on the Bible App with a group of ladies. It's a great way to further and create community among my sisters in Christ, and it was incredible. Ladies were opening up and sharing about things to women they didn't even know. It was absolutely beautiful. During the plan, there was one verse and one thought that stood out to me above everything: "there is no substitute for the presence of God."

"Here's the one thing I crave from God, the one thing I seek above all else: I want the privilege of living with him every moment in

*his house, finding the sweet loveliness of his face, filled with awe,
delighting in his glory and grace. I want to live my life so close to
him that he takes pleasure in my every prayer."*

(PSALM 27:4 TPT)

This is where the sawdust brownies come into play. Them there
brownies looked incredible. (I felt the need to use my best Carter County
sawmill voice). They were everything you dream a brownie should look
like, but someone had the bright idea they also needed to be healthy.
YUCK! Y'all, I don't do healthy I do tasty, and those brownies were lacking
the latter. Whoever had made the brownies went to extremes to substitute
all the goodness in the brownies with things like black beans and gluten-
free sawdust I mean, flour. In the process of substitution, they sucked the
goodness right out of them there brownies! But isn't that what we do?

God has given us himself. He has given us everything we need to feel
satisfied and fulfilled, yet we run to substitutions for our fulfillment. We
feel alone in our relationship, so we stay up all night watching unrealistic
Netflix romances or looking at pornography trying to fill the void only
building up more walls in our relationship. We struggle in our finances,
so we go shopping to make us feel better for a moment, only digging ourselves deeper into debt. We feel empty or worthless, so we try to find our
worth on social media, only to see everyone else's perfect Instagram is better than ours, sending us into a more profound depression and self-hate.

Do you recognize the cycle? When we substitute God for idols, we
lose. We lose our husbands, our friends, our homes, our worth, our faith.
There is no substitute for Jesus in our life any more than there is a substitute for brownies. You can run as fast and as hard as you want from God's
presence, but you will be empty and bound.

So I ask you, what are some areas of your life that you need to replace
the sawdust with sugar? What have you been using as a substitute for your
relationship with Christ? I pray that God searches your heart today and
reveals to you the places you keep hidden. Friend, I believe in you, and
Jesus is waiting for you. Go take back your life.

Daily Prayer:

Search me, Lord. Illuminate the dark places of my heart. Reveal to me the substitutions I've been allowing. God, I don't want to substitute you. Nothing compares to YOU and the goodness YOU bring to my life. Work in me and through me. In Jesus name. Amen.

*Shout out to my sweet friend, Faith Schweizer. She is absolutely incredible, and such an asset to this ministry and my life. And if you've never heard her sing, you should! Go check her out on iTunes. Thank you, Faither, for everything!

COMPARISON TRAP

My cousin, Jacob, and I have had an ongoing, yet innocent, battle over the latest gadgets for years. It usually starts with him purchasing the newest electronic and taunting me about it. I remember one year he and his wife had bought a flat screen television. (Back when that was the new thing, many moons ago.) It wasn't too long after that; I coveted what Jacob purchased. Weeks later, my husband and I set out to buy a new flat panel television; only I needed to one-up him, so I bought one that was one inch bigger. Ha! I showed him.

Now some of you are reading this thinking we've lost it. But I assure you we aren't too serious about this competition; it's all in good fun.

In 1 Samuel 8, we come across the story of the Israelites demanding a King. Until this point, they had never had a king. Samuel prayed to the Lord, and God granted the request despite the rejection that he was their King. While God listened to the people's demand, he did so with a warning from Samuel, about what it would mean to have a king (1 Sam 8:10-20).

> *"The people refused to listen to Samuel. "No!" they said. "We must have a king over us. Then we'll be like all the other nations: our King will judge us, go out before us, and fight our battles."*
>
> (SAMUEL 8:19-20 CSB)

"Then we will be like all the other nations."

This gripped my heart. Israel had a king God himself but they looked around at the other nations and were no longer satisfied with Him.

I realize the story I shared about Jacob and I is all for fun, but for a lot of us, its real life. God has graciously blessed us, but we look around at others and are unsatisfied. We see the new car in their drive, and our car seems a little dated; the new purse she carries, well, it sure didn't come from the Walmart clearance like mine did. Or worse, we look to another's marriage or children and pick apart everything wrong with ours. The comparison trap is a dangerous place to be. Our satisfaction will not be found in anything but Christ. Yet we allow the world to "woo" us through comparison with our neighbor.

Just as Israel ignored the cost of a king, we overlook the cost of comparison. Comparison can cost us financially, emotionally, and spiritually. It isn't above costing us our family, friendships, and our joy!

Please understand, God wants us to have a beautiful life, full of His blessings. He wants to bless us financially, emotionally, relationally, and spiritually. God meant for us to have astounding marriages, but not through comparison with others. He loves us and wants all these things for us, but the way to get God's gifts is by giving ourselves to Him! Can I take it a step further and say, when we are wholly His, we are content with what we have and we don't look so much to what our neighbor has.

"Seek first the kingdom of God and his righteousness, and all these things will be provided for you."
                                                                    (MATTHEW 6:33 CSB)

"I don't say this out of need, for I have learned to be content in whatever circumstances I find myself. I know both how to make do with little, and I know how to make do with a lot. In any and all circumstances I have learned the secret of being content—whether

well fed or hungry, whether in abundance or in need. I can do all
things through him who strengthens me."

(PHILIPPIANS 4:11-13 CSB)

Our contentment with, and in, all things can only come through
Christ. He is our strength when jealousy and discontentment well up. He
is our provider. Let's look to Christ to satisfy, and His blessing will follow.

Daily Prayer:

Lord, I don't want to be like everyone else. You have created me to
be unique and for a unique path. I don't want to shortcut my path
because someone else's looks better from where I stand. Give me
eyes to see that YOU are all I need and you are working in my life
to give me the best of you and what YOU have planned for me. In
Jesus name. Amen.

DAY FORTY-FOUR

EMPTY WELLS

A couple years ago, my brother, Kyle, was mowing his lawn when suddenly the earth beneath him swallowed the mower he was riding. I
can only imagine what was running through his mind as he tried to strad-
dle the giant hole while holding himself and his mower up from being
swallowed. As he told me the story, I couldn't help but laugh at the image
his story had painted in my mind. Curious, I wondered what could have
caused that? Oddly enough, it was an empty well. The well isn't opera-
tional anymore, and he has since covered it up. But as I thought about the
well, it made me think about the Samaritan woman.

> "He left Judea and went again to Galilee. He had to travel through
> Samaria; so he came to a town of Samaria called Sychar near the
> property that Jacob had given his Son Joseph. Jacob's well was there,
> and Jesus, worn out from his journey, sat down at the well. It was
> about noon. A woman of Samaria came to draw water. "Give me
> a drink," Jesus said to her, because his disciples had gone into town
> to buy food. "How is it that you, a Jew, ask for a drink from me,
> a Samaritan woman?" she asked him. For Jews do not associate
> with Samaritans. Jesus answered, "If you knew the gift of God, and
> who is saying to you, 'Give me a drink,' you would ask him, and he

*would give you living water." "Sir," said the woman, "you don't even
have a bucket, and the well is deep. So where do you get this 'living
water'? You aren't greater than our father Jacob, are you? He gave
us the well and drank from it himself, as did his sons and livestock."
Jesus said, "Everyone who drinks from this water will get thirsty
again. But whoever drinks from the water that I will give him will
never get thirsty again. In fact, the water I will give him will become
a well of water springing up in him for eternal life." "Sir," the woman
said to him, "give me this water so that I won't get thirsty and come
here to draw water."*

(JOHN 4:3-15 CSB)

The Samaritan woman had likely been showing up at this well for much of her life, drawing water each day, only to run back again and again. I'm sure the well felt mundane and old to her. I'd be willing to bet she dreamed of a system that would cause water to come to her from inside her home. She likely imagined everlasting water.

The day Jesus showed up in Samaria, He was there on appointment. Verse four indicates He had to go, but according to scripture, He could've gone around like most Jews would have done. Jews weren't exactly happy to be near a Samaritan, so they took a long way around to avoid them. But Jesus had to go through to meet a woman by a well.

If you continue reading in John 4, you find what Jesus had to offer interested this woman. But for her to draw from the well of Jesus, she'd have to stop drawing from the well she had always drawn from.

I'm sure the thought of drawing from a new well seemed scary and impossible. Married four times and living with a man, it's obvious she searched for fulfillment, but remained feeling empty. She had been trying to drink from an empty well and it left her thirsty. She wanted fulfillment but didn't know where to find it until Jesus rolled into town.

Maybe you too, have a well you've been drinking from, but it isn't satisfying like you had hoped. Perhaps it's a well of addiction, alcohol, or lust. Maybe it's over-eating, shopping, physical fitness, social media or finances. There are more wells to choose from today than ever before. I have been to some of these wells myself, and I can tell you from experience that they never satisfy. Only Jesus can give us the water that genuinely fills. Without His living water (John 7:37-38), we are not living we are only existing. Just as Jesus showed up to bring living water to the woman at the well, He came to do the same for you and for me.

What well are you drawing from? What well are you running to? Jesus is ready and willing to give you water that satisfies your every thirst. Will you drink from His well or will you continue to draw from empty ones?

"As the deer pants for streams of water, so my soul pants for you, my God."

(PSALM 42:1 CSB)

Daily Prayer:

I'm leaving the empty wells of life and chasing your living water, Lord. Remove my empty desires and replace them with YOUR desires. Save me from the dry wells that will swallow me up and drag me down. God, thank you that you have sent your Son to satisfy my every thirst and give me a new, better life. In Jesus name. Amen.

GOOD INTENTIONS

I proceeded up the stairs, patting myself on the back the whole way. I was so proud of how I handled the news they had given me. News that I didn't agree with, but determined to handle better than the last time. I had received similar news about a year before and didn't handle it so well. My goodness, was I super spiritual and loving at that moment or at least I thought. It turns out the other party seen things differently than I had.

In 2 Samuel, David, along with 30,000 troops, were transporting the ark of God from Abinadab's house to the tent which David had pitched for it.

> *"When they came to Nakon's threshing floor, Uzzah reached out to the ark of God and took hold of it because the oxen had stumbled. Then the Lord's anger burned against Uzzah, and God struck him dead on the spot for his irreverence, and he died there next to the ark of God."*
>
> (2 SAMUEL 6:6-7 CSB)

Now I'm willing to bet, Uzzah's intentions were pure when he reached out, but it makes me wonder if his heart wasn't.

As I read this story, I saw myself in Uzzah. I noticed how often, my intentions are good, but sometimes even with good intentions, I get it all wrong. There are times my heart and my intentions aren't on the same page. That night they gave me the news, I intended to love well and look like Jesus, but, I forgot to check my heart. My heart was broken, and I struggled to unite my heart to my intentions.

I know from experience, the struggle between loving people and speaking God's truth to them. The line between the two is thin. As Christ followers, we don't want to love so much that people think we are okay with any way of living, but we also can't go around Bible-thumping everyone, ultimately turning them off to Christ. I believe there is a time to speak the truth in love. But, the way to illuminate Christ in you, more often than not, isn't by what you say but it's how you live. Your life will always speak louder than your words.

That night, in my attempt to be spiritual and loving, I failed. Although I may have been truthful, I wasn't loving. My heart broke to know that not only had I hurt two people I love, but I didn't handle things the way Jesus would.

I encourage you to love like Jesus and extend grace like he does. He will tell you when it's time to speak a loving truth or when it's time for a lot of love. Sometimes in our attempt to do right, we just get it wrong. I am SO thankful for the grace God offers to us and others. In our good intentions, *"let's see that no one misses the grace of God." (Hebrews 12:15 CSB)*

Live Loud!

Daily Prayer:

God, I don't want people to see me as honest. I want people to see me as honorable. I can be honest all day long, but if I have no love, I look nothing like you. I want people to see me and know, while I may disagree with their choices, I will love them well. Just as you love the prostitutes, tax collectors, murderers and thieves. I too, can love those I disagree with. Help me see people through your lens and know when it's time to speak the truth in love. Help me love like you. In Jesus name. Amen.

GROW THROUGH

D o you ever go through the motions? Perhaps you've been through a situation, and you're doing your best to survive. Maybe you ask the question we all ask, "God, why am I going through this?" You put on your smile and do your best to shine your Jesus light, loud and proud; but it doesn't change how you feel on the inside. Maybe, God has spoken about a direction He has for you, but it seems like you will never get there. On your journey to the promise, you have hit one wall after another. Roadblock after roadblock. So again, you ask, "Why?"

I don't pretend to have the answer, why bad things happen other than we live in a fallen world. However, when I talk about why God allows us to go through things on the way to our promise, the fullness God has for us as individuals, I believe He's shown me, "why."

Some time back, my friend Faith and I attended a worship concert to celebrate our birthdays. It was an incredible evening, and I did a lot of talking and listening to Jesus. It was one of those times that I needed to focus on Him. Toward the end, Chris Brown of Elevation Worship, said something that struck me.

He stated, "the platform is not the purpose."

I loved what he said because being in ministry, it's easy to think it's about the platform. How many people am I reaching? Whats our church attendance? Eccetera. We get the mindset of, "If we don't have a big platform, we aren't doing something right, or we don't matter as much to kingdom work." But this is a lie and the absolute opposite of Gods heart. God doesn't measure the size of our platforms he looks at the measure of our obedience. I loved what Chris said, but it caused me to ask a question, "Lord, if the platform is not the purpose, what is?"

In the weeks and months to follow, I made it my prayer to understand what the purpose was. I thought, "maybe it's the people". The people we reach *has to be* the purpose. Just when I thought I had it all figured out, the Lord whispered something I didn't expect, like He often does.

He said, "Cassie, it's not the people."

What? It's not the people?

He whispered back to me, "It's the process; the process is the purpose."

That wasn't at all what I was expecting, or frankly, what I wanted to hear, but I let His spirit continue. He showed me: often we want to rush through the process, go through it, and move on to the fullness God has for us. Sometimes we even try to bypass this process, but God doesn't want us to just go through. He wants us to GROW through the process. I now understand that if the process is the purpose, then there's a purpose in the process.

As I let this marinate in my spirit, God brought King David to my remembrance. God anointed David King at a young age. 1 Samuel 16, tells the story of how it all comes about: Samuel sets out to anoint a new king one of Jesse's sons. He meets all the brothers and wants to choose Eliab (1 Samuel 16: 6).

> "But the Lord said to Samuel, 'Do not look at his appearance or his stature because I have rejected him. Humans do not see what the Lord sees, for humans see what is visible, but the Lord sees the heart.'"
>
> (1 SAMUEL 16:7 CSB)

DAY FORTY-SIX
_____

Let me stop here for a moment to remind you: you are enough! People may look down on you, they may reject you and they may set you aside, but God sees your heart. He knows what plans He has for you. No one and nothing, can stop the will of the Father! YOU. ARE. ENOUGH!

So, the Lord straightens Samuel out here, and directs him to ask if there are any more sons to choose from.

"Samuel asked him, 'Are these all the sons you have?' 'There is still the youngest,' he answered, 'but right now he's tending the sheep.' Samuel told Jesse, 'Send for him. We won't sit down to eat until he gets here.'"

(1 SAMUEL 16:11 CSB)

Again, I have to pause. Maybe you have been tending sheep for so long you wonder if you heard the Lord correctly. I get it, me too! I've been in the season of waiting, feeling like what He said about my life would never come to pass. Wondering if I missed it. But this verse reminds us that when we stay faithful where we are, God will send for us when His time is right. Stay steadfast in this season and God will bless your obedience.

Jesse sends for David, and in verse twelve, Samuel anoints David as king. The end. Just kidding. This was only the beginning for David. There was much for him to learn. It was 22 years from the time Samuel anointed David king, before he reigned over all of Israel. Say what? 22 years? Lord Jesus, that's a long time, am I right?! But God showed me this as a reminder that the process is the purpose, and there is a purpose in the process. So what use could 22 years of waiting have?

Well, plenty.

Playing the harp taught David humility (1 Samuel 16:14-18).

Fighting a lion and a bear taught David how to fight a giant (1 Samuel 16:34-37).

The giant, Goliath, taught David how to face an army (1 Samuel 16:49-50).

Saul's hunt for David's life taught Him to seek refuge in the Lord (1 Sam 22:1).

Shepherding his sheep taught David how to shepherd a nation (1 Samuel 22:11). The very position David was in when God called him King, was his biggest lesson his most significant growing experience.

> *"Do not despise small beginnings," meaning: don't hold them as insignificant because they are significant to the Father. What you thought was meaningless could be the very thing setting you up for greatness."*
>
> (ZECHARIAH 4:10 CSB)

> *"His master said to him, 'Well done, good and faithful servant. You have been faithful over a little; I will set you over much. Enter into the joy of your master."*
>
> (MATTHEW 25:21 CSB)

The purpose of the process boils down to growth. We are to *grow* through, not just *go* through things. Jesus would never allow us to go through something we couldn't grow through. We serve a good Father, and He wants only the best for us. Sometimes the best can come through a desert, a valley or the wilderness. These times are inevitable, but we get to choose: will we *go* through them or *grow* through them?

> *"Meanwhile, Moses was shepherding the flock of his father-in-law Jethro, the priest of Midian. He led the flock to the far side of the wilderness and came to Horeb, the mountain of God."*
>
> (EXODUS 3:1 CSB)

Did you catch that? On just the other side of the process the wilderness, the desert, the roadblock you're facing you will find the promise; the mountain of God. GROW THROUGH.

Daily Prayer:

Lord, teach me to not despise the small beginnings the process. When I don't enjoy growing through, send me encouragement to keep going. When this desert feels too lonely, minister to me. Surround me with your faithful presence. Send believers to lift me up and surround me. When I am discouraged by my lack, remind me your word is true and what you promise will come to pass. Teach me to have joy in the process. In Jesus name. Amen.

IN THE MIDDLE

A few years back, the kiddos and I took off to New Mexico to spend some much-needed time with Dustin. He'd been out-of-town working for several weeks, and I couldn't take it another second. We set off on our long, 18 hour drive to visit daddy. When we arrived, there wasn't much to do, so we ventured out in search of some fun. Our search led us to the famous Carlsbad Caverns.

Arriving at the Caverns, we were eager to get down in the cave and to see all of its wonders. We took the elevator down since it was the quickest and easiest way to get inside the cave. When we reached the bottom, we looked around and enjoying the beauty that was happening so far beneath the earth's surface. We loaded up on pictures and decided we'd better head to the elevator line; otherwise we may get stuck sleeping with the bats. When we returned to the elevators, the line had grown into a two-hour wait. With three kids, under the age of eight, we knew a two-hour delay would not work. So we decided we would take the 1.25 mile trail back out. "How bad could it be?" I thought. Well, it was awful; like the worst idea ever in the history of terrible ideas.

Just so you can get a glimpse of the trail I'm talking about, www.nps. gov compared it to hiking up a 75-story building. It was incredibly steep, and warning signs urged those with heart, back, and respiratory conditions to take the elevator.

Theoretically, we hiked up a 75-story building with three kids and one out of shape momma. At one point, in the middle of the climb, I lay sprawled out on the trail floor just trying to catch my breath. Strangers walking around me, while my husband and brother-in-law laughed. After an hour and a half (and lots of breaks), we arrived at the gate. We had made it to the top! I wondered so many times in the middle of that climb, if I would ever make it to the top; was there even a finish line to find? The middle is a hard place to be and a hard place to keep perspective.

As I write about the process, and how challenging it can be, it's essential to understand you have to keep pushing forward and grow through. The thought of growing through things is an encouraging thought, but how do I keep pushing forward in the middle of the process with no end in sight? How do I keep moving forward when I feel alone and sometimes even feeling abandoned by God? It's easy to see and believe that He's in the vision, the promise, the first step of faith and that He's there in the promised land, *when* we've finished the race. It's easy to see and believe He's in the beginning and that He's at the end, but why do we struggle to think He's in the middle?

"The priests who carried the ark of the covenant of the LORD stopped in the middle of the Jordan and stood on dry ground, while all Israel passed by until the whole nation had completed the crossing on dry ground."

(JOSHUA 3:17 CSB)

When I first read this passage it caught my attention and encouraged me. God nudged my heart and reminded me, He's in the middle. It may not always feel like it or look like it, but He's here right in the middle of my mess, my calling, my chaos and my journey to the promise. He will stay here as long as it takes for you, and for me, to get where He's leading us.

God doesn't call us and then abandon us; He goes before us, making a way a perfect way. If you are feeling alone, rejected and abandoned, maybe it's time to fix your focus. The middle can be scary and uncomfortable, just as it was for the Israelites when facing the flooded Jordan River. It's so easy to fix our focus on the flood rather than the Father, but He is here, right in the middle and He is making a way. Don't lose sight of the promise; fix your focus.

> *"It is the Lord who goes before you. He will be with you; he will not leave you or forsake you. Do not fear or be dismayed."*
>
> (*DEUTERONOMY 31:8 CSB*)

Daily Prayer:

Father, the middle is hard. Sometimes I feel alone and abandoned, but today I believe you are here, right in the middle with me and you won't move until it's time to move me. Uphold me with your mighty right hand in this time of hardship. Send other believers to me to encourage me and share their testimony of "the middle" with me. Lord, I love you and I trust you. Thank you for being with me, even here, in the middle. In Jesus name. Amen.

AWKWARD

B ack when I was a kiddo, my Step-Mom, Alberta, and I were at Walmart. We were doing our thing, shopping away when we ran into an old friend of hers. As they chatted, Alberta noticed she was rounder in the belly than the last time she saw her, so she asked what seemed fitting. When are you due? It seemed like an obvious question. Only, IT WASN'T.

The woman replied, "Oh, 'I'm not expecting."

OOPS!!! Talk about an awkward moment. I mean, really uncomfortable. How do you come back from that? Alberta was mortified, it was not her finest moment. She hasn't asked such a question since then. Lesson learned: never assume.

Have you experienced an awkward moment like that? Maybe you've said or done something, and it didn't turn out like you expected it would. I've had my share of them, but that one is my favorite. Mainly because it isn't my own (how convenient for me).

Reading through the book of Joshua, I came across a very awkward moment. Let me tell you, it's a whopper! But even in its awkwardness, God used it to speak to me. Maybe awkward moments aren't so bad.

"At that time the Lord said to Joshua, Make flint knives and circumcise the Israelite men again."

(JOSHUA 5:2 CSB)

Joshua just led the Israelites miraculously across the Jordan river, on dry ground, and that's when things get awkward. Joshua had to be thinking; "you want me to do what? Grown men will not take kindly to me hurting them like this. They are prone to hurt me if I come at them with a knife!"

Don't you know the Israelite men were thinking, "yeah, we'd like to hear from God ourselves on this one."

Imagine, (or don't), but it must have been super awkward for everyone.

What in the world does the circumcision of grown men have to do with us? Well, I'm glad you ask. As I read verse two, it occurred to me, sometimes in the process of our promise, God may ask us to do some awkward things. He may ask us to do something that, frankly, we don't want to do; but for us to walk in our promise, we have to do the hard things and the "not so fun" things. Despite how it looks or how we feel about it, we have to learn to obey God's every word.

Joshua could have said, "no, this is too uncomfortable for me" (and for them), but he would give up the promise both for himself and the Israelites (Joshua 5:3-9). We too have the choice to say "no thanks" to the hard things, but it could mean forfeiting the promise. If things are looking awkward on your journey to the promise God has for you, don't give up. God has a great plan. It may get a little uncomfortable, but your obedience will bring about many blessings. Don't quit on the process, because it *will* lead you to the promise.

"And through your offspring all nations on earth will be blessed, because you have obeyed me."

(GENESIS 22:18 CSB)

Daily Prayer:

Lord, there have been many times you have nudged me to do some uncomfortable things, and I've turned you down. No one enjoys being uncomfortable. God, today, I think back to the uncomfortable sacrifice you made on Calvary to save someone like me. Today I choose to be uncomfortable, even if things get a little awkward for me because I want your favor and your promises for my life. Lord, don't hold back from me. I'm ready to live in the fullness, no matter the cost. In Jesus name. Amen.

You're the Good

"Nazareth! Can anything good come from there?" Nathanael asked.
"Come and see," said Philip.

(JOHN 1:46 CSB)

This scripture shocks me. The "anything good" that they were referring to was Jesus. I realize Nathanael didn't yet know Jesus, but from my perspective, I'm like, "hello, he's talking about Jesus, the Messiah God's own Son!"

It shocks me that even Jesus wasn't exempt of ridicule over where He was from. Sounds familiar, doesn't it? That's the world we live in, where we decide people's worth based on where or who they come from. I've been there. People looking at me and saying, "can anything good come from Ellsinore, or from Debi and David", (my parents)? I'm guilty myself of having said similar things about others.

Sweet sister, we have to get to where we don't value one person any more than we do another. God looks at each of us with the same set of love. To Him, it doesn't matter where we came from, who our parents or grandparents are, what we've done or who we've been - our worth is the same. Our value is equal. When God created us, He said that we are good (Genesis 1:31). So who are we to determine someone's worth?

How can we make a change? How can we value every life? I say, we start with Phillip's response to Nathanael. *"Come and see."*

Jesus had asked Phillip to follow Him, and Phillip extended that invite to Nathanael. Such a simple, yet profound thought. Let's get to know others and the God who made them. When we grow closer to Jesus, our love for others will also increase; we will see the worth of others through the lens of Christ. No more placing limitations on our neighbors. In Christ, there is no limit on their worth or the good they can accomplish through Him.

What if you struggle more with believing *you* are good? Maybe you've been labeled worthless or inadequate. It's easier to believe God can use your neighbor and that they have more value than you do because of where or who you've come from. But let Paul remind you of this truth,

"For we are his workmanship, created in Christ Jesus for good works, which God prepared beforehand, that we should walk in them."

(*EPHESIANS 2:10 CSB*)

Notice scripture doesn't say we should walk in them if we come from the right region, country, state, family, or if we've never made mistakes. NOPE. You are His child, and you are good. God created you for good works. Before you were born, He knew you and was already preparing your path. Stop believing the lies of the enemy or the lies that people are filling your mind full of, that nothing good will ever come from you, your family, or your region. You, my friend, are the good. Embrace it, and all God has for you.

Daily Prayer:

Father, you are good. Thank you for creating me and putting inside me a purpose for good works. You believe in me. When you made me, you deemed me "good". You have found so much good in me and you have adopted me as your daughter. Fill my heart and my mind full of your truth and your love for me. I am good, and I have your power within me to display your goodness to the world. In Jesus name. Amen.

THE CLIMB

Dustin and I have this weird thing where we name our vehicles. He has a truck, (a truck that's nearly as old as we are), we call her Brownie. Brownie is, well, in "rough shape". It's one of those deals where you just say a prayer, get in and go. Faith gets her from point A to point B most days.

A while back, I had the privilege (or something like that), of driving Brownie. However, I do my best to stay away from her as it takes "unique" skills to drive her. While she got me to where I needed to be and back, I wondered if we would make it to the top of the last hill before our home. The 20 mile round trip was quite a journey, but my adventure in Dustin's 1990 Chevy pickup, caused me to think of our faith journey to the "mountaintop".

Mountaintop experiences are my favorite (amen?). I don't care too much for the valley or desert seasons. I love it when all in my world is right and thriving. I'm guessing you do too. I believe it comes naturally to most of us to want to live on the mountain where everything seems so right. However, I also think the journey to the mountaintop is so incredibly beautiful. Difficult, but beautiful.

The climb to the top can feel lonely, stressful, long and exhausting. Often, wondering if you've taken the wrong path. There are times you will crawl because your strength to walk is all but gone. I know this doesn't sound beautiful, but it is. It's the climb where our faith stretches, and we grow. It's where we learn to lean on and trust God for the provision and for the promise that awaits us. The process to the top prepares us for the peak. The process causes us to appreciate the mountaintop when we finally arrive. I've sat atop one physical mountain in my life and I can tell you the drive up was less than fun; but when I saw the sunrise above the clouds, it was breathtaking and worth the journey to the top.

I don't know where you are on your spiritual adventure, but this is my advice to you: Don't despise the climb. It is part of the process of something far more magnificent than you can ask or imagine (Ephesians 3:20). The Lord is with you every step of the way (Deuteronomy 31:6).

> *"The Lord my Lord is my strength; he makes my feet like those of a deer and enables me to walk on mountain heights!"*
>
> *(HABAKKUK 3:19 CSB)*

Daily Prayer:

Father, thank you. You have provided for me on this long journey. You have allowed me to draw ever so close to you each day. Although the process can be less than fun, and I enjoy the view from the mountaintop, I understand there is much beauty to see along the way. It's on the climb, that you are helping me and making provision for me. It's on the climb I experience great and mighty miracles. Thank you for going alongside me on this journey. There is no one else I'd rather climb with. In Jesus name. Amen.

THE HIDING PLACE

Hide and Seek: one of the greatest games of all time. I can remember countless hours of playing this game with my siblings, cousins and friends. Still today, I watch my kids enjoy the game. The difference between then and now is, my kids have 40 acres, a trained German Shorthair they cheat with, and a four-wheeler to navigate on; I had a bicycle and a small yard. Their hiding places are endless; mine were limited. If you ever found a great place to hide, you wouldn't dare tell anyone because then everyone would use it.

As I was pondering this thought of the hiding place, I thought back to my youngest brother, Lane. When I was a teenager, I loved the horror movie, Scream. Why you ask? I'm not sure, but I did. So, being the great sister I am, I would let Lane watch this film with me. I was almost 17 when he was born, so by age two, he was watching Scream with me. What was I thinking? Poor kid. It's a wonder it didn't rot his brain. Anyways, as Lane and I would watch "the Scream," as he called it, he would hide his face under the covers every time the masked man would appear. He hid until I promised it was over. He found the sheets to be his hiding place; Lane's safe place from the Scream.

Isn't this you and I? Chaos breaks loose in our lives, and we frantically look for a hiding place a safe place to turn. I think it's natural. When you hear tornado sirens, you don't wait on your front porch to greet it; you run to your basement or cellar a hiding place from the storm. In life, you will face chaos. Hard times, hurt and painful experiences will come. You will want a hiding place, a safe place to gain strength and get your bearings. I encourage you to have a hiding place, but my encouragement begs the question: where is your hiding place?

Some time ago, I went through a situation that knocked the breath out of me, spiritually. I needed a safe place to catch my breath, regroup my thoughts and rest for a minute. I sought refuge from the storms of life and I remembered David with his hiding place.

So David left Gath and took refuge in the cave of Adullam. When David's brothers and his Father's whole family heard, they went down and joined him there. In addition, every man who was desperate, in debt, or discontented rallied around him, and he became their leader. About four hundred men were with him.

(1 SAMUEL 22:1-2 CSB)

David was on the run from Saul because he was jealous of David and wanted to see him dead. So David, amid a lousy situation, sought a hiding place. Did you notice that when others heard, nearly 400 men who needed a hiding place joined him? The cave was a place where a bunch of broken men gathered to recover, catch their breath and regroup. So, what was so special about this cave? Nothing. It wasn't the cave that rescued David, but the God in whom he took refuge in. It wasn't a place he found comfort in, but the Lord whom he invited into the cave with him.

David wrote both Psalm 57 and 147 while in the cave of Adullam. Let's check them out.

"Have mercy on me, my God, have mercy on me, for in you, I take refuge. I will take refuge in the shadow of your wings until

the disaster has passed. I cry out to God Most High, to God, who vindicates me. He sends from heaven and saves me, rebuking those who hotly pursue me- God sends forth his love and his faithfulness."

(Psalms 57:1-3 CSB)

"Praise the Lord. How good it is to sing praises to our God, how pleasant and fitting to praise him! The Lord builds up Jerusalem; he gathers the exiles of Israel. He heals the brokenhearted and binds up their wounds. He determines the number of the stars and calls them each by name. Great is our Lord and mighty in power; his understanding has no limit. The Lord sustains the humble but casts the wicked to the ground."

(Psalms 147:1-6 CSB)

David may have found a cave to hide in, but he took refuge in God. I don't pretend to understand what you are going through, but no matter how small or how significant it may be: God is the perfect hiding place. Often, we want to run to relationships, shopping sprees, alcohol, drugs, and other empty places for refuge when life happens. I encourage you today: Run to the Father. He endured the cross to save you— to make you whole and holy. If you need a place to hide, hide in the Almighty.

"You are my hiding place; you protect me from trouble. You sur-round me with joyful shouts of deliverance."

(Psalm 32:7 CSB)

Daily Prayer:

Father, I need a place to hide and I choose to run to you. Life is kicking my tail and I'm tempted to run to empty places. I now understand running to empty places will not help me, but only cre-ate more chaos. As I run to you, lift me up, help my broken heart and bind up my wounds, as you promise you will. I abide in you. In Jesus name. Amen.

BEFORE THE FALL

Pride: a feeling or deep pleasure or satisfaction for one's achievements.

I struggle with this word, "pride", from time to time. I bet you have too. Take heart though. Pride has been a fight for people throughout the ages, dating back to old testament times. Take King Uzziah, for example.

King Uzziah was 16 when he became king of Judah. Can you even fathom an election where a 16-year-old child ran for president? It blows me away to think of someone so young having such power.

At the time Uzziah was crowned king, 2 Chronicles 26:5 says, *"during the time that he sought the Lord, God gave him success."*

He had great success as a young king, but it didn't last forever. By the time we reach verse 15 and 16, scripture says, *"So his fame spread even to distant places, for he was wondrously helped until Uzziah became strong. But when he became strong, he grew arrogant, and it led to his own destruction.".*

Uzziah acts unfaithfully toward the Lord and ends up with leprosy.

As I read this story, a couple things jumped out at me. First was verse five, *"during the time he sought the Lord."* That tells me there was a time he chose *not* to seek the Lord. When we are pursuing God, He will faithfully bless us. God gave Uzziah success in every area and He wants to do the same for us. The problem isn't that God stops blessing, it's that we stop seeking.

"Seek first the kingdom of God and all these things will be added to you."

(MATTHEW 6:33 CSB)

The second thing that stood out to me were verses 15 and 16, *"until he became strong."* He became so accomplished throughout the land, he decided he didn't need God. Maybe, in his own mind, he was enough; he could handle 'whatever' by his own strength. I know for me, I can get in the mindset that I can do things on my own. It's easier than you may think to allow self to take the place of the Lord in our life. When we become strong, we weaken Christ in us.

"Pride comes before destruction and an arrogant spirit before a fall."

(PROVERBS 16:18 CSB)

King Uzziah was going places and doing mighty things with God's blessing. But the moment he stopped seeking God and started pursuing self and the applause of man, all that ended. No matter how great we may become, we can never stop chasing God and His will. God did not call us for the applause of man. But it's all about the glory we bring the Father.

My dear friend, Faith Schweizer, wrote and sings a song called Audience of One. She wrote about how we are to make Jesus famous in our lives, not ourselves. Faith sings, I write, and *we* live for an audience of one. Don't allow pride to steal your promotion in kingdom business.

Daily Prayer:

Father, I want to make you famous in my life. God, I want nothing that isn't of you. Search my heart, dig deep, and remove the root of pride. Lord, may I only live and serve for an audience of one: you, Lord. There is nothing you have called me to that I can handle by my strength. Make me strong through my weakness. My hearts cry is when others look at me, they see you. In Jesus name. Amen.

WINTER BLUES

I am an ardent lover of summer. Give me 90 degrees, beautiful views, the water, and I'm a happy girl. Some of my favorite things are t-shirts, shorts, flip-flops and ponytails. I could spend all day, every day, just soaking up the sun. Summer time makes me smile. My love for this season is a large part of why I dream of a vacation home in Hawaii. I mean, summer forever, right? Never again having to drag out the dreadful winter clothes or my winter blues.

COUNT ME IN!

Now, as much as I'd love to stay in summer or spend forever on an Island in the Pacific, that just isn't reality in my current stage of life. So, I live in here in Missouri where the weather is wildly unpredictable. You may think I've lost it. Maybe you prefer fall or winter. Despite our preferences, we live in a world of many seasons. Seasons of weather and seasons of life. I can escape Missouri's crazy weather by flying to Hawaii, but I can't avoid the unpredictable seasons of life.

> *"There is an occasion for everything,*
> *and a time for every activity under heaven:*
> *a time to give birth and a time to die;*
> *a time to plant and a time to uproot;*

a time to kill and a time to heal;
a time to tear down and a time to build;
a time to weep and a time to laugh;
a time to mourn and a time to dance;
a time to throw stones and a time to gather stones;
a time to embrace and a time to avoid embracing;
a time to search and a time to count as lost;
a time to keep and a time to throw away;
a time to tear and a time to sew;
a time to be silent and a time to speak;
a time to love and a time to hate;
a time for war and a time for peace."

(ECCLESIASTES 3:1-8 CSB)

Maybe you're in a season of raising toddlers, or you're the caretaker of the ones who raised you. Maybe your season is more of a financial one—you've landed your dream job or your career has crumbled. Perhaps, it's an emotional season— you've just had a baby or have lost a loved one. I don't know what your season looks like, but as I read the words in Ecclesiastes, I'm encouraged that I'm not alone. We've all been through times that were great and times we 'couldn't wait to get through. It's not the great times that are most difficult to endure. We can get stuck in those seasons, being too weary to move forward. We question if this season will ever end. Your season is complicated but it *will* change; seasons ALWAYS change (Genesis 8:22). There's a time for everything, and joy will come in the morning (Psalm 30:5). Let's not allow this harsh season in life to keep us from missing the next great one.

My Pastor often says, *"If it's not good, it's not over."* (Romans 8:28).

If I can encourage you: don't just endure this season, but explore it. Ask God to teach you right where you're at. What can you learn from your current situation? How can God use this for good? How can this season help you show mercy and grace toward others? I have been through those hard seasons, so I'm not trying to make light of what you are going through. Instead of trying to run away from the craziness, can we take some time and build a snowman? Take a moment to embrace this season and learn from it; you won't be here forever. The pain, the hurt, the tears, the discouragement— they only last for a season.

Daily Prayer:

God, thank you that this is just a season of life. Lord, help me not to bypass the winters of life but embrace them as an opportunity to draw closer to you and learn from them. Give me provision for this time in my life, equipping me for this season. Lord, I wait expectantly for a warmer season. I know it's just around the corner. Thank you for seasons and that I don't have to stay here. In Jesus name. Amen.

LOOKING IN THE REARVIEW

I read a story about a taxi driver in India by the name of Harpreet Dev. 30-year-old Harpreet is known for his reverse driving skills. In his story, he tells us it happened by accident. He had been driving his Fiat Padmini, and it had gotten stuck in reverse late one night.

"I was outside the city and had no money, so I thought of driving the car backward until Bhatinda," he said. "Then I drove backward and later on I gained confidence."

He gained enough confidence driving in reverse became the only way he drove. At the time they published the article, he had been driving backward everywhere he went for 11 years - pretty impressive. While Harpreet's driving won him some fame in his hometown, it came at a price - he now suffers from severe back and neck problems.

He admitted, "I have got a severe backbone problem from driving so fast in reverse because my whole body gets contorted."

I'll admit, Harpreet sounds almost as fascinating as Tow Mater from Disney's film, Cars. After reading Harpreet's story, I couldn't help but think about how much he sacrificed by looking back. Looking in the rearview cost him physically and he would suffer the rest of his life all for a few years of fame and fun. Isn't it so easy to get stuck looking back when God's called you to move forward?

"The sun had risen over the earth when Lot came to Zoar. Then the LORD rained on Sodom and Gomorrah brimstone and fire from the LORD out of heaven, and He overthrew those cities, and all the valley, and all the inhabitants of the cities, and what grew on the ground. But his wife, from behind him, looked back, and she became a pillar of salt."

(GENESIS 19:23-26 CSB)

God blessed lot and his family allowing them to flee from the wicked city of Sodom and Gomorrah before God brought destruction upon it. Verse 17 says, *"As soon as the angels got them outside, one of them said, "Run for your lives! Don't look back and don't stop anywhere on the plain! Run to the mountains, or you will be swept away!"*

So they ran. They headed out, but Lot's wife looked back.

I looked up the Hebrew for "looked back," and it means more than to look over one's shoulder. It means "to regard, to consider, to pay attention to". I believe Lot's wife hadn't left the city, at least not in her heart. God graciously called her out, but in her heart, she hadn't left, and it cost her. Looking in the rearview stopped Lot's wife in her tracks and she could not move forward anymore. The past she wanted so much, robbed her of the future God had planned for her.

I can't tell you how many times my past life, past mistakes and past hurts have tried to keep me from moving forward. But, I decline what *was,* for what *can be.* May we be women who run for our lives and not look back! Trust God is leading you to something new and better. He only wants the very best for His daughters, so let's not get caught looking in the rearview.

Daily Prayer:

God, help me keep my eyes forward. Help me look ahead to all things you have planned for me. There are many things you have called me out of, and I don't want to forfeit my future by looking back. My family, my friends and my fellow sisters are counting on me to move forward. Keep my eyes set ahead. In Jesus name. Amen.

HOLD TIGHT

T oss and turn, toss and turn. I lay there wide awake, my mind spinning in circles battling and wrestling with my thoughts; the situation surrounding me and the Lord. Maybe you've been there before; up all night wrestling through your conflicts, whether physical, emotional, or spiritual. Some nights feel like a WWE match in my mind. I wake up exhausted and without progress, only to fight the same battle again the next night.

After my last battle of the mind a few nights ago, I decided, ENOUGH IS ENOUGH. I'm done letting the situation win. Tonight, I'm not giving up until the Lord takes it from me; until I'm able to surrender the battle entirely. My determination led me to the story of Jacob in the book of Genesis.

"Jacob was left alone, and a man wrestled with him until daybreak. When the man saw that he could not defeat him, he struck Jacob's hip socket as they wrestled and dislocated his hip. Then he said to Jacob, "Let me go, for it is daybreak." But Jacob said, "I will not let you go unless you bless me." "What is your name?" the man asked. "Jacob," he replied. "Your name will no longer be Jacob," he said. "It will be Israel because you have struggled with God and with

men and have prevailed." Then Jacob asked him, "Please tell me your name." But he answered, "Why do you ask my name?" And he blessed him there."

(GENESIS 32:24-29 CSB)

As I read and reread this scripture, it drew me to verse 26: He said to Jacob, *"Let me go, for it is daybreak."*

But Jacob replied, *"I will not let you go unless you bless me."* Jacob had a lot of wrestling to do because of his past life as a deceiver. When day broke, he could have given up and let go of the fight, but he refused to let go until God changed him.

This idea challenged me and I wondered, "am I willing to hang on, fighting until I'm changed? Or will I give up at daybreak only to face the same fight again and again?"

Maybe you enjoy the fight, but I am tired of the tossing and turning. The battles that rage inside my mind and my heart, the situations that never improve: I'm tired of revisiting the same fight night after night, day after day. I want change to happen in my circumstances. I want change to happen in my life. I want a blessing, but to receive change and a blessing, I have to hang on to Jesus and not let go until change happens. We can't give up at daybreak because it's easier, we must hold on and not let go.

What keeps you up at night? What are you giving up on? What battle do you continually fight? Is it an addiction, shopping, food or relationships? Maybe it's an unending struggle with your spouse or a struggle with depression. Perhaps you're fighting for the promises and dreams God has put in your heart. I don't know what you're wrestling, but I know you can't let go not this close to a breakthrough, a blessing. Sister, God wants to give you a new name, a new identity based on what He sees in you; not based on your issues, your past or your situation. However, this requires you to fight until you receive what you are fighting for and what God has for you.

Don't give up.

Daily Prayer:

God, you created me to be a fighter, and that's just what I plan to do. Lord, I refuse to quit. I refuse to give up this close to a breakthrough. God, I am grabbing hold of you and I am not letting go. Lord, change me and bless me. In Jesus name. Amen.

SEEMINGLY INSIGNIFICANT

L unch at Burger King that day seemed pretty insignificant. We'd done it a hundred times before, but little did I know how much life would change sitting at a table for two and munching down chicken nuggets.

Maybe you've experienced a seemingly insignificant moment. A moment that seemed almost routine or mundane, but then surprised by the significance it held. Well, that was me on November 26, 2003. I was working at the front desk of Comfort Inn and I really enjoyed the position other than I didn't get to spend much time with Dustin, as he was working out of town back then. At the time, we were dating, but that day he had shown up to my work over the lunch break and asked to take me to lunch. I ran to the back, begging my boss, and he obliged. Soon we were out the door and off to eat. Dustin was super sweet and gave me the choice of a nice meal, but I was craving some chicken nuggets smothered in salt, just the way I like them. With little convincing, we headed off to Burger King. Had I known what was coming, I would've picked somewhere fancier, but my seemingly insignificant lunch had me convinced it was just another day. That it was until I pulled my engagement ring out of his coat pocket. So right there, over chicken nuggets loaded with salt, and a room full of retired people seeking the senior discount, Dustin asked me to be his wife.

There are so many times in life I have been guilty of taking the little things, or the small beginnings, for granted. I see this so much in my life and within the church. It's almost as if a title becomes more significant than the work does. Dustin could have chose to wait on the engagement because of the setting, but for him, it wasn't about where he was, it was about who he was with. I could have gotten upset because he asked me to marry him at a fast-food restaurant, but it wasn't about that for me. We could have been standing in a dumpster, and I would have said "yes". (Although I'm glad it wasn't a dumpster.)

Maybe your "seemingly insignificant" moment is cutting grass for a company you want to run someday. I say, keep cutting. God may use this opportunity to do something incredible. Perhaps you'd love to run the women's ministry at church, but your current role is janitor. Small beginnings, my friend. In this season of life, just do the work set before you. Do it well and in time, and if it matches God's heart for you, you will run women's ministry, run the company, speak at conferences, write the book, marry the man of your dreams, etc. Just because *it*, (whatever it is for you), seems insignificant, it doesn't mean it is.

Friend, keep moving forward. I am here rooting for you. God, too, is cheering you on and making a way through what seems impossible. Don't give up.

> *"Do not despise these small beginnings, for the Lord rejoices to see the work begin, to see the plumb line in Zerubbabel's hand."*
>
> (ZECHARIAH 4:10 NLT)

Daily Prayer:

Father, open my eyes to the significance in the seemingly insignificant moments. No longer take for granted the little moments that appear so small. Just as a child begins as a baby and grows into an adult, so do the things you set in my heart. Today Lord, I will be patient with the seemingly insignificant, because in due time, they will become far more significant than I can imagine. In Jesus name. Amen.

MORE THAN A CONQUEROR

"Who shall separate us from the love of Christ? Shall trouble or hardship or persecution or famine or nakedness or danger or sword? As it is written: "For your sake we face death all day long; we are considered as sheep to be slaughtered." No, in all these things we are more than conquerors through him who loved us. For I am convinced that neither death nor life, neither angels nor demons, neither the present nor the future, nor any powers, neither height nor depth, nor anything else in all creation, will be able to separate us from the love of God that is in Christ Jesus our Lord."

(ROMAN 8:35-39 CSB)

Y ou are strong, you are brave, you are fierce, you are capable, you are enough, you are loved, and you are more than a conqueror!

Too often we let ourselves to get bogged down by the weight of life, we believe what the enemy whispers to us. We get overwhelmed and worn out. We buy the lies we aren't enough to get it all done and get it done decently. (Amen?!) For me, it's the constant and overwhelming struggle of juggling being a wife, mothering three kids, homeschooling, ministry and being a good friend and sister to others. There are days I do it well, and there are days I believe the lie; the lie that says I'm not enough and I'll never be able to do it. Perhaps for you, you are a college student who faces school each day and real life each night. Struggling to study and spend time with the ones you love most. Maybe you're a momma to toddlers and feel you'll never be able to accomplish anything again; you're trapped between dirty diapers, and sippy cups. I've been there too, friend. Single, married, young, or old; whatever your season looks like, I want to remind you of this truth: you are more than a conqueror.

God created you to kick butt and take names! Nothing and no one can stop what God started in you. Sure this may be a difficult season to flourish in one area or another, but it's coming. In the meantime, keep moving forward. Keep kicking Satan in the face, keep kicking down the roadblocks he throws your way. Keep fighting. You are a fighter, and you will win the war within. When you get knocked down, and you believe the lies, remember that God loves you. He is proud to call you daughter. Nothing can separate you from His love.

If that's you, and you're knocked down today, as God extends His mighty right hand to you. I also am extending my hand to you. Let's get you up, dust you off, and get back to winning this war! God has incredible things ahead for you, but it requires you, (and me), to move forward!

Daily Prayer:

Father, I'm moving forward. I believe your words over me and I will go to war. I am enough because you have made me enough. When I feel like giving up and when I feel beat down, I will remember that through you, I am more than a conqueror. In Jesus name. Amen.

IT'S NOT ABOUT YOU

Would you consider yourself a dreamer? I'm a dreamer. God has given me big dreams that, frankly, seem crazy and that I can never accomplish without His mighty hand in the middle of them. I love that He's put ideas inside of me, entrusted them to me, but I am not the only one. He made you a dreamer, too. God created each of us with a gift and a dream to use this passion He's etched in our hearts. Maybe for you, it's writing a book, owning a business, being a homemaker, speaking, singing or adoption. We all have a dream inside of us. Sometimes our dreams get buried under our burdens, but they are there. Dreams are part of our gift and our call as Christ followers to tell the world about Jesus. With our ideas, come responsibilities and temptations. Temptations convince us our dreams are about us, but it's our responsibility to make them about God.

"God's big dreams for us are not about us at all."

— Kyle Idleman

"What we do for the kingdom involves us, but it isn't about us."

— Megan Norman

God gives us big, impossible dreams to chase. Not because we're better than the next person, or more qualified. Most often, it's the opposite. He gives us big dreams to chase because He understands that big dreams mean greater glory for Him.

David was a little shepherd boy, and it brought great glory to God as a little shepherd boy defeated a giant and became King. Moses had speech problems, yet led an entire nation. Joseph had a big dream, but spent time as a slave and a prisoner. In the end, taking a position that saved his family and brought great glory to God. God chose you for your dream, so if you are feeling less than qualified, it's because you are; but God is more than adequate, and through you, He will gain great glory!!!

If our dreams aren't about us, does that mean God won't bless us? Not at all, God *wants* to bless us. But blessing hinges on our obedience to Him and His will for us. God longs for us to live a full life in Him, but don't mistake His *big* dreams for *your* big glory. God's desires for you are not about you. It's all about Him, and along the way, with obedience and a humble heart, God will bless you too. He will cause favor to pour out in your life for your humble obedience to Him.

Whatever dream God has put inside of you - chase that thing down. Bring our King BIG glory. Follow God's heart for you, even if it sounds insane, (and sometimes it will). Don't sit back because you're afraid to fail or worried you aren't what God is looking for. The all-knowing knows what He's doing, and He's picked you out of billions of people. So, set self aside, and face some giants. The bigger the giants, the bigger the glory God receives!

"For everything comes from him and exists by his power and is intended for his glory. All glory to him forever! Amen."

(ROMANS 11:36 NLT)

Daily Prayer:

Father, I'm grateful that what you've gifted me with has meaning. I'm thankful my passions have a purpose. Lord, as I step out in faith, I pray you give me confidence that only you possess. Step with me, walk with me and cover me as I step out. I am putting to work all you've put in me. Give me a fresh vision and direction for the ideas you've given me. Open doors and make connections. Lord, I am excited to jump and I'm grateful you saw fit to choose me. Humble me. In Jesus name. Amen.

DAY FIFTY-NINE

JOURNEY TO THE PALACE

Being a dreamer, I always have a long list of ideas. Some of them are God given, others are likely more selfish. Either way, my list is long. I'm sure we are all full of dreams if we took the time to consider it. Dreams or visions are beautiful things to have (Proverbs 29:18). Dreams and ideas give us hope.

"Where there is no vision, there is no hope."
— George Washington Carver

Being the dreamer I am, I have to be very careful about comparing myself to others living in similar dreams. It is easy for me to get a little jealous when I see someone else fulling their dreams, when mine seem so far away. I have to remember not to compare myself to a seasoned writer of 20 years and expect to be where they are. It's great to want to be a better writer and strive for that, but I can't forget she too has a writing journey. I don't know what she's gone through to get where she is, but I know it didn't happen overnight.

As I thought about my dreams of writing, among other dreams, God reminded me of Joseph's journey.

Like many of us, Joseph had a dream. One night he dreamt that he would rule over his brothers. The vision did not make his brothers thrilled. He was already their father's favorite, and now he's dreaming of ruling over them. Josephs brothers hated his dream, and The bible says, *"they hated him even more."*

They hated him so much they plotted to kill him. Threw him into a pit in the wilderness and left him for dead. While they sat down to eat, they saw a caravan coming in the distance and decided that, rather than kill him, they could sell him and make a profit. Apparently, the going price for a Joseph in those days was 20 pieces of silver. So they sold him and ran off with their profit. I'd love to tell you the story gets better for Joseph, but it's only just begun. Soon after being sold into slavery, they sold him once more, this time in Egypt to Potiphar an officer of Pharaoh and the captain of the guards. Life is going from bad to worse; I'm sure his dream must've seemed foolish. As time goes by, Potiphar's wife lies about Joseph and they throw him into prison for an "attempted rape" he didn't even commit. But God still had a dream for Joseph, just as He always had. Joseph ended up interpreting dreams for Pharaoh and eventually became second in command. Only Pharaoh, the king, was more significant than Joseph.

I say all that to ask you this: do you think Joseph would have chased the dream God gave him if he had known ahead of time all he would go through in the process? Would you?

This story helps me remember that dreams and visions have a process. When we look at others ahead of us on the journey, we must not envy them, for we don't know what they have gone through to accomplish the vision. I pray that on your journey to the palace, it won't be as painful as Joseph's journey; but even if it is, remember that the process will lead you to the promise. In the palace, lives changed. Joseph saved a nation and his family from within the palace, but it was the process to the palace that put Joseph in the perfect position to do so.

I encourage you to fix your eyes on the way-maker our God, who guides our steps. Don't look to others with jealousy because their path may not be one you're willing to walk down. Take the path laid out for you and don't grow weary of the process, for it will perfectly position you for the palace!

Daily Prayer:

Father, thank you for your dreams and ideas. But more so, thank you for the journey I get to take— the walk that brings me closer to you and teaches me perseverance. God, help me not to grow jealous of my sisters, but to celebrate her journey and her promise. There will come a day when things align just as you want them, and the dreams you birth inside of me will come to pass. On that day, I want my sisters celebrating the brave journey I have walked. Guide me. Give me the courage to keep moving forward despite what I may face along the way. In Jesus name. Amen.

DAY SIXTY

VISION PRODUCES HOPE

"No one gets to tell me how big my dreams can be."

— Rachel Hollis

These words echo inside of me. I'm such a dreamer. In my marriage, parenting, finances, and ministry; EV-ER-Y-THING. There isn't one area of my life that I don't dream big about.

But this often comes with the weight of many naysayers. I'm sure people hear me talk about my dreams and plans and think, "girl, you don't have what it takes."

They may be right, maybe I don't have what it takes, perhaps I've lost my mind. But this is what I know for sure: if I allow all the negative voices that speak into my life to overrule God's voice, and my own, I will fail every time because I will never even try. (Haters gonna hate, ya'll!)

Other people do not get to tell me how big my dreams can be, and they don't get to discourage my vision. So, I want to challenge you today. If you have an idea and it honors God, go for it and don't give up. If you are the naysayer I talked about, encourage someone and stop being afraid to dream yourself. Often, when we discourage others on their journey, it's because we are scared of our own or jealous of theirs. Don't be *that* voice. Instead come alongside your sister, encouraging her and rooting for her;

when you do that, you'll soon discover a dream of your own, and they'll be there to support you.

"Where there is no vision, the people perish."

(PROVERBS 29:18 CSB)

I love this scripture. Why would the people perish without a vision? Because without it, there is a lack of hope. Dreams and ideas give us something to hope toward. Our hope in Christ is what saves us from drowning in a storm. It holds us together in a crisis; it's that hope toward something greater. Our God-given dreams are a hope toward something bigger, so don't let anyone steal that from you. I believe God created us to be dreamers, not to replace our hope in Him, but to lean *into* Him while He dreams up big ways to impact His kingdom through us. Know this: if God put a dream inside of you, girl, you better believe that nothing and no one can stop what He has started. Dare to dream, sweet sister.

My prayer over you today is this:

Father, thank you for this sweet lady. Thank you for the opportunity to walk this journey together. God, I pray as she closes this book and moves on to the next that you will cause her to remember YOUR truths that were tucked into the pages of this book. God, go with her on her faith journey, encourage her, comfort her, empower her with your strength to chase you and live wholly for you. Be her first thought and her last thought each day. Give her dreams and visions and the provision to make them happen. God, thank you for allowing me to pour into my sister.

In Jesus name. Amen.

ACKNOWLEDGMENTS

To Dustin, my best friend and husband, thank you for the unending love and support over our 19 years together. You are my biggest encourager when chasing crazy dreams. This project was no different. Thank you for being patient when I sat for hours at my computer and taking up the slack when the house became a wreck. You are one of a kind, and I am so thankful you are mine. I love you.

To Wyatt, Annah, and Tyler, thank you for believing in me and supporting me in more ways than you know. Thank you for sharing in the excitement about this project and being so quick to understand when writing took over. You three are the best and God has the best in mind for you. Keep chasing Jesus.

And to my team, Faith Schweizer, Angela Rogers, Mom (Debi Reynolds), Paige Kerr, and Angie Chism. I've heard it said that teamwork makes the dream work, and I believe this more now than ever. Working with you ladies has been a dream itself. Your constant devotion of time and prayer have meant more to me than you will ever know. You five beauties are the best, and I am so grateful for your investment in my dream. I know God will reward you in your dreams for investing in mine. I can't wait to see what He has for each of you.

Thank you to all the gracious people who read this book before its birth and shared feedback and helpful thoughts. I am forever grateful for your hard work helping make this dream a reality. A special thank you to

Jim Laudell for your mentorship throughout this project. Our talks have been such an encouragement, and I can't thank you enough.

Jacob Smith, my brother from another mother, my father in the faith. Thank you for countless hours over the course of my life that you have spent pouring into me, pushing me closer to Jesus with each conversation. You will never know the impact you have had on me. Thank you for always following Jesus, it's because of you, I follow Him too.

And last but not least. I couldn't have made this book happen without the support of the Elm Hill family, my family, and friends; thank you for believing in me and being the first to grab your copies. Your support means everything.

CPSIA information can be obtained
at www.ICGtesting.com
Printed in the USA
LVHW041302061020
668084LV00008B/21